Professor Robert Bor is a Chartered Clinical, Coun... ...alth
Psychologist registered with the UK Healt... ...so a
and Couple's Therapist, regi... ...ncil
...chotherapy. He works ther...  ...le
...ildren who have a range of ...s,
... ... and families, drawing on ...and
...dynamic ideas.

...in the NHS he is a consultant psyc... ...ogist at the Royal Free Hospital,
...don. He also has a busy private psychology practice and is co-director
...namic Change Consultants (www.dccclinical.com) which offers
...ogical therapy to people as well as executive coaching to leaders in
...te sector. Rob is a child psychologist and consults to three leading
... - St Paul's School, the Royal Ballet School and JFS, all in London. He
...he consultant psychologist at the London Oncology Clinic and the
... Clinic, both in Harley Street, and provides psychological services
...oms Healthcare in the City of London. Rob has a special interest in
... psychology and in treating people who have a fear of flying.
... has published more than 25 books and 150 academic papers on
...lling and therapy. He consults to private clients and organizations
...hout the UK and internationally.

...Gill is an accredited BACP and BABCP psychological therapist. She has
... ...for over twenty years as a therapist and for the past ten years in the
...roup Practice in north London and in the London School of Economics
...litical Science. She has trained in a range of therapeutic models. Her
...t and expertise is in using evidence-based and brief approaches to
...er patients cope better. Currently she is interested in the application of
...ilness-Based Cognitive Therapy ideas, as a means of promoting self-
...id healing. She is the co-author of a number of books on the theory
...actice of therapy. Her most recent publication is *Counselling in Health*
...ettings: A Handbook for Practitioners (Palgrave, 2009).

...Stokes is an accredited BACP counsellor, and also has a large training
...pervision practice. She is a director of, and tutor with, Online Training
...recent years Anne has concentrated on:
...ning counsellors to diploma and master's level at the University of
... tol, and also training post-qualification counsellors to diploma level
... Online Counselling;
- working with large and small organizations to provide counselling
  support and manage change and transition;

- developing a successful independent counselling and supervisory practice, both face to face and online;
- outplacement counselling to offer practical and psychological support to employees affected by organizational change and redundancy;
- designing and implementing training programmes and workshops in conjunction with organizations to meet specific employee development needs.

Anne has written a number of articles and contributed chapters to several books. She has recently co-authored *Online Counselling: A Practitioner's Guide*, published by Palgrave in 2009. Anne lives in Hampshire and works throughout the United Kingdom. She has a master of science degree (Counselling Supervision and Training) from Bristol University and an MBA from the International Management Centre, Buckingham.

Overcoming Common Problems Series

Selected titles

A full list of titles is available form Sheldon Press,
36 Causton Street, London SW1P 4ST, and on our website at
www.sheldonpress.co.uk

Overcoming Common Problems Series

Overcoming Common Problems Series

Therapy for Beginners
How to get the best out of counselling

ROBERT BOR, SHEILA GILL and ANNE STOKES

First published in Great Britain in 2011

Sheldon Press
36 Causton Street
London SW1P 4ST
www.sheldonpress.co.uk

The author and publisher have made every effort to ensure that the external website
and email addresses included in this book are correct and up to date at the time of
going to press. The author and publisher are not responsible for the content, quality or
continuing accessibility of the sites.

British Library Cataloguing-in-Publication Data

A catalogue record for this book is available from the British Library

ISBN 978–1–84709–103–1

1 3 5 7 9 10 8 6 4 2

Typeset by Damco Solutions Ltd.
Printed in Great Britain by Ashford Colour Press

Produced on paper from sustainable forests

*This book is dedicated to our patients with whom
we have had the privilege to work and to their families,
and to everyone thinking about or who has been
referred for psychological therapy.*

Contents

Acknowledgements

We are grateful to Margaret Oakes for her help with Table 4.1, and to Dr Carina Eriksen, CPsychol, for contributing some ideas on the section on relaxation in Chapter 10.

1

Introduction

Therapy? Counselling? Psychology? Psychiatry? If you are reading this book, you may be one of the hundreds of thousands of people in the UK who are thinking about having psychological therapy to help you to get over or cope with a problem. Or maybe you have been referred for therapy or counselling by your doctor and want to know more about what lies ahead. You may be feeling uncertain, confused and possibly overwhelmed or frightened about embarking on a course of counselling or therapy. Perhaps you have practical questions about how to find a therapist; what to expect; how to prepare yourself; how to choose the right therapist for you; or what will happen in the therapy session. Some uncertainty and apprehension or even fear of what lies ahead can be made worse by the fact that the personal problem you had in the first place has possibly also dented your normal self-confidence and ability to deal with personal problems.

If you find yourself nodding in agreement with anything that you have read so far, then this book could be what you are looking for at this time. It can help guide you through the delicate process of understanding

- what therapy is about;
- what brings people to therapy;
- what the differences are between therapy, counselling, psychology and psychiatry, as well as some of the main approaches used;
- which problems can be dealt with in therapy (and which can't);
- how to find or choose a counsellor or therapist;
- what you need to know about the therapist and her approach before starting with her;
- what your counsellor or therapist may need to know about you;

1

- how to 'read' some of your own psychological problems and feelings and begin to understand how to overcome them on your own, before starting therapy;
- why you may feel vulnerable and frightened about meeting with a therapist;
- what you can do to prepare yourself for therapy so that it can work better, and possibly more quickly, for you;
- what to do to help yourself or where you can gain self-help support – such as via the internet or through books – to get you started.

This book is aimed at you, the reader, someone who may be thinking about having therapy. It is also for the friends and relatives of people experiencing challenges or difficulties in their lives who may want some ideas about how to get that individual to see a therapist. This book will answer many questions that potential clients raise about therapy, including how it works and whether it is appropriate for your problem. The book has four main aims:

1 to help you recognize when a personal difficulty has become a psychological problem that might be helped by therapy;
2 to help you gain a balanced view of which problems can be treated through therapy and how therapy can help;
3 to help you consider what changes you can initiate to try to help overcome your problem by yourself, which may mean that you can put on hold the need to see a therapist;
4 to help you best prepare for therapy.

Therapy is becoming increasingly popular in most Western countries and cultures. This book is relevant to a modern work-driven era, where people may have become disconnected from family, supportive friends or religion. Therapy is now an accepted means to overcome or cope with numerous life difficulties and challenges, alongside psychiatric treatment as well as holistic approaches.

By now you will have noted that we use the terms 'therapy' and 'counselling' (as well as 'therapist' and 'counsellor'); nowadays these are mostly regarded as interchangeable and mean the same thing or the same person. Both counsellors and therapists seek to work therapeutically with their clients whichever title they adopt, even if they sometimes use different approaches and skills. We will explain more about this in Chapter 4 of this book. For greater ease of reading, we will use both terms throughout the rest of the book. We will also refer to therapists as 'she' and clients as 'he' (unless it is the opposite gender being referred to in a particular illustrative case). These are simply convenient pronouns, as clients and therapists can obviously be either gender.

Therapy is an activity that occurs behind closed doors. Public understanding of it is mostly gained through hearsay and media representations. We will try to de-mystify the process of therapy as much as is possible in this short practical book. The objective is to provide clarification for you, the prospective client considering undergoing therapy or intimidated by the prospect, so that you can better understand how it works, its benefits and also some limitations. It aims to empower you by helping you to gain a clearer sense of what happens in therapy so that you can become an active participant in the process of your therapy – including choosing a therapist – thereby maximizing its beneficial effect.

A small note of caution: therapy should not be undertaken lightly. At times, psychological therapy may be seen as the panacea for many problems in modern society, whereas in fact it may not always be useful or appropriate – e.g. in solving a practical problem such as housing or financial difficulties. There are numerous challenges and potential pitfalls in finding a therapist and preparing yourself for the process. Indeed, just at the time when your emotional vulnerability is likely to be at its greatest, you may need to put your trust and confidence in someone and talk about personal and sometimes emotionally painful concerns. It is important to exercise good judgement and care in seeking appropriate psychological support.

Choosing a therapist and starting therapy should be carefully considered *before* embarking on it, whether it is your own idea to have therapy or the suggestion of someone else. If you are thinking about having therapy, you may want, at the very least, to inform yourself about what you can expect and emotionally prepare yourself for the experience. You may also seek to explore what type of therapy would suit you the best. Preparing yourself for therapy can help to avoid the experience inadvertently becoming a costly – in terms of both money and time – and emotionally distressing mistake which could merely compound your difficulties.

Modern approaches to therapy seek to have realistic aims and goals. In our busy lives, the most appropriate model for the delivery of therapy for the vast majority of those who need or seek it, is that it should be something you easily access and from which you can benefit at different stages of life or when confronting new problems. Just like consulting your GP from time to time about health issues, so therapy could have an intermittent role in your life when the need arises.

This book describes mainly practical self-help ideas and hints. You may feel sufficiently helped by the ideas shared, or the pointers at the end for helping yourself, that you may decide you have gone some way to solving your problem without the need for therapy. We have tried to express our ideas in jargon-free language and to avoid 'psychobabble'. A wide range of issues and topics are covered in the following chapters. Some are listed in Box 1.

Box 1   Key questions

Key questions that will be answered include:
- How do I know if therapy might help?
- What is therapy?
- Is therapy always about revisiting my childhood?
- What main approaches to therapy are there?
- What do I need to know to choose a particular approach?
- How do I choose a therapist?
- How long will therapy take? What might it cost?
- Which problems can be treated through psychological therapy? Which cannot?
- Do I need therapy?
- What can I do to help myself?
- How do people feel before they start therapy?
- What can I expect to happen in a therapy session?
- What can I do to prepare myself for therapy?
- How will I know whether I am making progress?

You may be reading this book for one of several reasons. Perhaps you are considering therapy for yourself, either in relation to a problem you are experiencing or in order to gain a deeper understanding of some issues or concerns in your life. You may also be interested to learn more about what therapy is and how it can help people generally. Perhaps you are curious to know when it can be helpful in people's lives and find out about some of the main approaches that are used in therapy. Another reason you may be interested in this book is that you have wondered how it feels to be in therapy. Your interest may be more practical, and you may need help in how to choose the right therapist for you or to match a therapeutic approach with the difficulty or problem that you are facing.

We hope that you will find the contents of this book not only useful but also informative, whether or not therapy is for you personally or for someone you know. All three authors are committed and experienced therapists. Each of us has more than twenty years' full-time experience as therapists, working in a wide range of settings and with many different people who experience different problems and issues in their lives. We are strong advocates of therapy because we believe that it can make a difference in people's lives. We have seen how it can help people, alleviate distress and improve insight into coping with life's difficulties.

We are also mindful of some of its limitations and of some of the stereotypes that abound that may influence thinking about therapy. Some of these limitations are more evident in situations where there is a mismatch between a client's expectations and what therapy can provide. The limitations can also present when the needs of the client are not met by either a therapist or a particular therapeutic approach. In many situations, these are avoidable difficulties.

Preparing yourself for therapy can, however, be more difficult in a situation where you may be experiencing psychological distress as you may feel less clear in your mind about how to make decisions about sensitive matters such as choosing a therapist. Again, we hope that this book will help guide you through this process and increase the likelihood that therapy can work better for you.

We have one final aim. As practising therapists, we recognize the value and importance of clients undertaking some therapeutic work outside sessions, on their own. In the modern era, almost all of us have access to the internet, books, self-help material, support groups and organizations, and specialists such as doctors and nurses, as well as the support of friends, families and colleagues. In the 'old days' of therapy more than ten years ago, all therapeutic work was reserved for face-to-face sessions with your therapist. Nowadays, things are different and there is a significant amount that you can do, both between sessions and even before you embark upon therapy, to help yourself. This book contains some ideas that can help you to work therapeutically even before you have met with a therapist. We offer guidance and invite you to reflect on a wide range of issues so that you can be better prepared for therapy, and indeed be able to start the process of change for yourself.

2

Aims of therapy

It's unhelpful to keep repeating the same behaviour or thinking the same thoughts and yet expect something different to happen. This is what many people do when they go on feeling low, miserable or stressed. Nothing is going to change until you try something different . . .

The pressure that Western competitive society places on us constantly to achieve can contribute to a sense of failure and increase stress. Nothing ever seems to be 'enough'. We may feel pushed to the next step or to procure the next more spectacular model on the market, but this pressure can deplete a person of energy and resources. Social and personal relationships can be neglected or sacrificed. This can lead any one of us to experience a profound sense of isolation, emotional distress and a myriad physical symptoms, leading to a visit to the GP for help. Taking the step to see the doctor may be all the more difficult because emotional distress may be viewed by others as a sign of failure, which can make matters even worse.

Therapy can provide the context for you to pause and reflect, to be still, to find your own voice, to access your own desires, fears and aspirations, to confront your worries, distress or grief. It is a way in which you can solve specific problems. In the professional and confidential setting that therapy provides, you can feel free to express your thoughts and feelings without the need to defend your point of view. The strength of this context lies largely in the fact that the therapist is a trained professional – someone who is essentially a stranger to your world. Her only objective is to attend to you, carefully to hear your story, to respect your point of view and not to judge or criticize. Such a context can be profoundly impactful as it will be very different from most of your normal daily interactions with other people.

People seek therapy in order to explore personal difficulties or issues they may be encountering. These may be specific problems such as difficulties in a relationship or fear of public speaking. Perhaps you feel that you would like to improve your understanding of how you think, feel, relate and manage your life. You may also be thinking about therapy because you may wish to gain a deeper understanding of some feelings that you may be experiencing; it can help you to gain clarity and a sense of confidence in overcoming a difficulty if you have improved insight into the nature of the difficulty and your response to it. You may also be thinking about therapy because you want to get more out of your life.

There is a wide range of reasons why people find therapy helpful at different points in their lives, as Brett's situation illustrates (note: this case is based on a real situation but is heavily disguised to protect the client's confidentiality).

> Brett, a 38-year-old teacher, knew that the news was not good when his father told him that he had been diagnosed with pancreatic cancer. Over the months, he witnessed his father deteriorate from being a strong, healthy and vibrant person to someone who was clearly suffering from advanced cancer. His father became increasingly bedridden and would spend bouts of time in hospital for treatment and also in a hospice for convalescence. Brett found this very stressful. He had always enjoyed a close relationship with his father, making this change more difficult to bear. He knew that his father was likely to die, and in spite of this knowledge and his understanding of what lay ahead, he did not feel that he could cope well with the feelings he was having. He was unable to work for a week because of the nausea and low mood that he was experiencing when thinking about his father. He knew that there was nothing he could do to change the course and outcome of his father's illness, but he also knew that he needed to be strong and supportive for his father. Brett's best friend suggested that he see a therapist in order to help him to come to terms with his father's advancing illness and the inevitability of his loss. Through seeing a therapist Brett found ways of learning to cope better with his father's illness and eventual death.

It is not always easy to clarify what you want to gain from therapy. It is, however, an important first step to take; without some understanding of what you want to gain, you may find it more difficult finding the right person for you and, equally, choosing the right approach.

There are similarities and differences between the many therapy approaches that are practised. Some of these are discussed in the following chapters. It is useful, however, to think in terms of the broadest goals that therapy can help you to achieve. Therapy should be transformational in that it changes some of *what you think*, *what you feel* or *how you behave or react*. It should be able to help you with at least one, or all, of the following aims:

- to better understand and sometimes change unwelcome feelings you are having;
- to live better with a particular problem, even if the problem itself cannot be changed or overcome (for example, if somebody is diagnosed with a life-threatening condition, therapy may not have an impact on the course of the illness but it can help the person to live better with that illness, or with the illness of a loved one, as in Brett's case);
- to deepen your understanding of patterns in how you relate to others;
- to facilitate personal change, if this is what you need and want;
- to change the way you react in situations or in response to a problem that you have identified.

Therapy *cannot* change what has happened in your past, though it can change how you think and feel about what has previously happened to you. It can help you have a better outcome to a problem that you have had or are currently facing. Malcolm's anxiety is an example of a problem that can be successfully treated in therapy.

Malcolm was a 29-year-old salesman who had enjoyed a normal life until recently. One day, when he was in a large supermarket, he suddenly felt sweaty and nauseated. He noticed that his breathing had become rapid and his heart was beating noticeably more quickly than normal. He felt light-headed and worried that he was about to pass out. He abandoned his trolley and made his way back to his car. He was able to open the door and sit down and within a few minutes was able to calm himself down. He felt shaken by the experience and worried that he might have been having a heart attack. He was able to get an emergency appointment with his GP, who examined him. Fortunately, his doctor was able reassure him that he had not had a heart attack. Instead, she felt that he had probably experienced a panic attack. She explained to Malcolm that a panic attack can feel like having a heart attack but that it is not normally caused by an underlying medical condition. Their conversation then turned to Malcolm's personal life. His GP enquired as to his general stress level. Malcolm said that he had been under pressure at work due to the recession and needed to improve his success with sales. He had also booked himself a flight to the Canary Islands for the Easter break. However, he had never been much of a confident flyer and the thought of getting on a plane worried him, although he had tried to put it out of his mind. His GP explained to him that in all likelihood, the stress of his job and the fear that he would be on an aeroplane within a few weeks had triggered a panic attack. She referred Malcolm to the practice counsellor, assuring him that the counsellor would be able to help him to cope better with his panicky feelings.

Identifying and defining your issue or problem

Your therapist will ask you at the start of the first session what you are hoping to gain from your meeting or course of therapy with her. This is another way of asking what the problem or difficulty is that you wish to address. Perhaps this is something to which you have already given a lot of thought. Your concerns or worries about having your problem may have left you feeling distressed as a result of having to cope with this difficulty. Changes in family circumstances are a common trigger point for distress which may lead to a referral to see a therapist, as was the case for Alex.

Alex had recently turned 17 and had been thinking for some time that he needed to see a therapist. The reason for this, he thought, was because seven years earlier his parents had separated and subsequently divorced. This did not cause him undue stress at the time as he accepted that his parents were unsuited to each other and they had prepared him well for the separation. However, his father subsequently remarried. His mother, in turn, started a relationship with another woman. While Alex said that he had no problem with his mother having a lesbian relationship, he felt that his mother's partner took no interest in him at all. He had a sense that his mother's partner hated men and particularly disliked children. In his experience, this was an unhelpful family arrangement. He very much wanted to leave home and go and live with his maternal grandmother, with whom he had a very close relationship. His parents had differing views as to whether he should leave the family home. Nonetheless, Alex felt that he would like to talk to a counsellor because he somehow lacked self-confidence in spite of his maturity and insight. He felt that his self-confidence was low and led to him underperforming at school and also being self-critical. He was unclear as to how much these feelings were influenced by his family situation or by other circumstances and he felt a need to gain a deeper understanding of what was happening. He saw his school counsellor, who in turn referred him for longer-term psychological therapy in order to help explore these issues and difficulties that he was experiencing.

Therapy usually works best when:

1 you have identified an issue or a problem (or a wish to explore life issues more deeply) which you would like to address;
2 you need help in working out what is making you feel stressed out;
3 you are motivated to deal with or overcome this problem;
4 your expectations and uncertainties about what may happen in therapy have been addressed and explored at an early stage in the professional relationship;
5 you know what to do to prepare yourself for therapy and how to get the most out of it.

Therapy happens in different settings

Therapy is carried out in many different settings, and the issues about which you seek counselling will sometimes be influenced by the context in which it happens. Some people see a therapist privately, while others may meet with a therapist in a work context or an educational setting. In many countries, therapy increasingly happens in a medical context such as a hospital or a GP's surgery. We now know that at least one out of every three patients that a GP sees has some psychological or emotional difficulty. So GPs and other health care professionals – nurses, health visitors, speech therapists, physiotherapists – along with non-medical professionals such as employers and pastoral care staff in schools, colleges and universities, are trained in identifying when it may be appropriate for you to meet with a therapist. These professionals will usually be very happy to discuss with you the decision to see a therapist. If therapy has been suggested to you by your GP or another professional it is certainly worth considering such advice seriously. An interesting statistic suggests that 85 per cent of people suffering from depression visit their GP complaining of a physical symptom.

Questions you may have about therapy

How can talking help?

Talking through a problem can be very helpful in disentangling your feelings about the situation that is currently bothering you. A skilled professional will help you to get a different perspective on things and can help you work out what your next step should or could be.

What can I do to prepare myself for therapy?

Therapy works best when you are ready and motivated for it. It involves both thinking and doing. This book will provide many suggestions for you to try out to improve and enhance your chances of getting the most out of a session of therapy. It may be that when such suggestions are implemented, your mood sufficiently improves and you begin to feel better to the extent that you may decide not to see a therapist. 'If it ain't broke, don't fix it!' is probably sound advice. This book will help you to work out at what point it would be beneficial to talk to a therapist.

What if I feel embarrassed?

A therapist is a trained professional experienced in talking about very personal and private issues. These are not shared with anyone without your permission. Registered therapists must all abide by a professional code of conduct.

How can I find a therapist who is right for me?

Later on in this book – see Chapters 4 and 5 – we provide some guidance about the main approaches to therapy that are practised and what approach can be used for different problems. We also provide advice as to where you may locate reputable practitioners.

How can I know what kind of problem to discuss with a therapist?

It is best to understand the nature of the therapy process as a shared activity between therapist and client. The subject of the therapy conversation can in principle be anything that you want to address, or that upsets you. The nature and causes of problems that can cause emotional distress are many and varied and so are the problems people bring to therapists. In the next chapter we describe the kinds of issues or problems people experience that may prompt them to think about having therapy.

3

When is it helpful to see a therapist?

Introduction

Everyone experiences ups and downs in the course of their life. This is normal and arguably healthy. It is what makes us real people. It is often what connects us all together in that we share some of these mood swings. If, however, we are feeling stressed out or unhappy at times when other people appear to be enjoying their lives, it can make us feel disconnected and apart from others. This in turn can give rise to uncertainty, fear and physical symptoms, as well as a loss of confidence. Experiencing mood swings or feeling worried or anxious about 'not feeling your normal self' can only make the whole experience worse. It would be unrealistic, however, to expect to be always in the same mood and have the same feelings in every situation throughout our lives.

The purpose of this chapter is to outline those problems, issues, concerns, circumstances or simply particular moments that commonly prompt people to see a therapist. People manage stress differently for a great variety of reasons. Personal circumstances vary greatly, and people have very different thresholds for psychological or emotional distress just as they do for the endurance of physical pain – a person's response to pressure is completely individual. It is therefore not possible to be definitive about reasons people see therapists, but this chapter should give you an idea of the more common ones in order to help you see whether counselling might be appropriate for you.

In this chapter, we have included some vignettes which illustrate some of the personal difficulties experienced by people we have worked with. We have shared these because they serve to illustrate some of the range of problems that people experience, which have prompted them to see a therapist. They also highlight the diverse nature of these difficulties and the unique and special circumstances that may account for their cause or onset. All the cases below and throughout the book are based on real situations, but we have disguised all the identifying details. For example, none of the names of cases relate to any clients with whom we have worked and most of the clinical details have been altered. Nonetheless, the nature of the problems described is real and some of these may have personal relevance to you when reading them. Lucy, for example, found that her mood changed after she had her first child.

> Lucy sought psychological counselling two weeks after she was discharged from hospital having given birth to a beautiful baby son. This was her first child and she was filled with expectation and joy at the prospect of starting a new family. However, things did not turn out as she had anticipated and within a short period of time she started to feel depressed. Lucy found it difficult to get up in the morning and found it very stressful feeding her child, who seemed difficult to console. While she had good support from her mother and her partner, she still felt alone emotionally. She became increasingly weepy and lost her appetite. Somehow, the joy of having a child had not materialized as she had imagined. A friend with whom she attended antenatal classes had suggested that she sought psychological counselling to help her understand her feelings with a view to helping her to cope better with her low mood. Her friend told her that she might be suffering from postnatal depression, and while Lucy had heard about this she was reluctant to attribute it to herself. Nonetheless, she took her friend's good advice.

Lucy's situation illustrates the two main situations in which people are likely to see a therapist. The first is to find help for a problem that they are experiencing in their life. The other is as a means to explore and understand feelings, motives, unconscious processes, behaviours and patterns of behaviour in a wide range of situations where such matters may benefit from exploration – in other words, to understand 'what makes them tick'. For many, the idea of going to see a therapist stems from advice or a referral from another professional, colleague, friend or family member. The most frequent and obvious example of this is a visit to your GP for health reasons that prompts your doctor to suggest that psychological counselling could help you to deal with a particular symptom or set of personal circumstances. Occasionally, too, this can come from other sources or settings, such as a teacher at school, a university tutor who recommends a child or a student to see a counsellor, or a lawyer who may recommend counselling to help a couple cope with separation and divorce.

It is worth remembering that therapists have different areas of expertise and that many different approaches to therapy exist, since this influences the process of identifying problems or issues for therapy. The differences between therapists and how they work will be discussed more fully in Chapters 4 and 5 to help you decide on what approach may be most beneficial for your particular situation.

Therapists can help to clarify the problem

It is worth keeping in mind that you do not need to be absolutely clear about what the problem is or if therapy is the most suitable form of help before setting up a first meeting with a therapist. A problem in one part of our lives can impact on many other areas of our lives which may result in a sense of feeling overwhelmed and confused about what the main problem is. There is no need to worry if this is your situation. Every experienced therapist should be able to help you feel sufficiently at ease in a first therapy session, however stressed or confused you feel. It may, of course, take more than one meeting to figure out what the problem is and whether therapy is right for you now. When Michael came to see a therapist he was not sure about his real reasons for feeling so low.

> Michael had come to see a therapist as he had been feeling upset and close to tears for some months. Two years earlier his 'healthy' son had been diagnosed with a genetic defect for which there was currently no medical treatment. Michael's work was suffering. He had begun to arrive late at the office as he was often called upon to care for his son in the night. As a consequence, he had been threatened with dismissal. Michael also confessed that he was very concerned about his marriage relationship. His wife too was distressed. He said that the two of them

had begun to bicker, they had given up on their social life and their relationship had begun to deteriorate. Michael also admitted that he had begun to drink too much alcohol as a way of hiding from the hard reality of his life. He was feeling overwhelmed and did not know where to begin to resolve his problem. With the therapist's help Michael was able to identify that the grief associated with the thought that his child could not live a normal life was at the heart of his misery. Although this issue was a deeply painful one for Michael, it gave the therapist a starting point that felt real, focused and relevant to Michael.

Being too clear about the problem may not always be helpful

If you are feeling very 'stuck' about an issue or a problem this may contribute to feelings of hopelessness and to the belief that there is nothing you can do to change the situation you are in. Many circumstances can at times seem insurmountable. Sometimes people believe that the cause of their stress lies with other people and not within themselves, and this can contribute to the belief that talking with a therapist or anyone else cannot possibly change anything about the situation. Such feelings of hopelessness or even despair may in fact be a good indication that speaking with a therapist might be beneficial. This was the case for Richard.

Richard had been feeling trapped and miserable for a number of months, but when his GP suggested that he should talk to a therapist he was very reluctant to do so. Richard said that he was very clear that his problem was his boss and he did not see how talking to a therapist could change that fact. Eventually, he agreed to the idea and explained to the therapist at their first meeting that his boss was critical and volatile and was making his life a misery. Richard said that whatever he did, his boss criticized it. The therapist asked a number of simple questions, such as 'How long has your boss been critical of your work?' 'Has this always been the case?' and 'Was there a time when your boss was supportive of your work?' Richard then began to recall that his boss had not always been critical of the work that he produced and had actually praised him on some past occasions. The criticism that he was currently experiencing from his boss had only begun about six months ago, just at the time that Richard had begun to get bored with his work and, by his own admission, had begun to produce substandard work. When Richard began to think about his work situation more carefully he started to realize that his boss was being an effective manager. She was simply doing what she was paid to do by being alert to below-average work by those she managed. At this point in the conversation, Richard was beginning to feel more hopeful about what he could do to change his situation.

There are probably as many different problems as there are people who bring their difficulties to therapy! While there are categories of problem, such as 'addiction', 'stress', 'trauma', etc., their very nature, intensity and impact is always a very personal and unique matter. One of the great advantages of modern psychological therapy is that it is tailored to help you understand your difficulties within your own unique context. Your therapist will treat you as an individual whose unique circumstances and experience of the problem need to be clearly understood.

The list below includes some of the kinds of difficulties that you, or perhaps someone you know and care about, may be experiencing. We have grouped them together for ease of reading, though some may be related to other problems too.

Worries, stress, anxiety and fears

- You feel afraid, anxious or phobic (such as a fear of flying or a fear of leaving your home).
- You are aware of irrational fears that something bad could happen to you or to a loved one.
- You experience 'free floating' anxiety, which like butterflies in the stomach but for no apparent reason.
- You feel agitated or restless and cannot explain this.

Low mood and depression

- Your mood is down.
- You are feeling that you do not take pleasure in activities and relationships that you used to enjoy.
- You feel that you are not in control of some of your thoughts, which may seem irrational, intrusive and persistent.

- Your interest in sex has decreased.
- You feel angry and can sometimes act in this way, possibly for no good reason.
- You feel irritable or grumpy.
- Your thoughts have become very negative and you can't seem to be able to shift them.
- You are struggling to cope with some of the demands of life.
- You question the purpose of life and have considered ending your life.

Coping with change, physical problems and loss

- You are going through a loss and experiencing feelings associated with grief which are difficult to bear.
- You have worries about your health or have been diagnosed with a medical condition and are experiencing stress in dealing with the condition and its symptoms.
- Your sleep and appetite are affected due to stress and worry.
- Your weight has fluctuated for no apparent reason, suggesting that you are either gaining weight through overeating or losing weight by not eating carefully enough (this may be a sign of worry, anxiety or low mood, among other possible causes).

Relationship and sexual difficulties

- You keep repeating unhelpful patterns in relationships, whether these are with your partner, friends or work colleagues.
- Problems in a relationship do not seem to go away, causing you emotional distress.
- Your sexual interest has declined or you have specific sexual difficulties (pain during intercourse; premature ejaculation in men, among other problems).

Addictions or substance misuse

- You rely on or are addicted to alcohol or recreational drugs.
- You may feel that you are addicted to certain activities, such as gambling, the use of the internet, pornography or overeating.

Recovering from a past traumatic experience

- Events and/or circumstances from your past, such as your childhood, are playing on your mind and affecting your confidence and esteem.
- In the past, you suffered a traumatic event such as emotional or sexual abuse, an accident or a natural disaster, which has continued to affect you in unpleasant and negative ways.

The list could go on for several pages, but these are the main reasons that people think about therapy for themselves. However stressed or distressed you may feel, it is important to acknowledge that it is a positive first step to recognize your difficult feelings and to act on them by thinking about seeing a therapist. You can take comfort in the fact that almost everyone experiences at least some of these feelings at some point in their life.

There are three important factors that may influence your decision as to whether you should seek therapy:

1 whether you feel that you can cope with these feelings;
2 how long they have been going on – the longer they have been present, the more likely they are to remain with you;
3 the strength or intensity of these feelings if they are uncomfortable and unwelcome. Even though the unpleasant feelings may last for only a short period of time, they may be so unpleasant that having them is on its own disturbing and frightening and therefore may make you think towards therapeutic support.

If you have been experiencing some or many of the feelings described above over a sustained period of time, it is usually a good idea to arrange to have a health check by your GP in order to rule out any physical condition that may be making you feel below par. It is especially vital, if at any time you have thoughts about ending your life or harming yourself or anyone else in any way, that you arrange to see your GP before making an appointment to see a therapist.

Therapy can help you to understand the source or cause of your distress, work towards making it easier to bear and, hopefully, overcome it, whether it is a problem 'within' you, or one triggered by external events, such as in relationships, as Tyra experienced.

Tyra was distraught and felt traumatized when she discovered that her husband had been having an extramarital relationship with another parent from school. She discovered this by chance because her best friend had told her that there had been rumours at school about her husband's relationship. When she confronted him he denied having an affair, which made her feel even worse about the situation that she faced. She felt confused about how things had been in the relationship and whether she had somehow contributed to her husband's infidelity. She also felt that it might have been her fault because she had not wanted to have an intimate relationship with her husband for the past year because of health problems. Tyra felt that she needed to talk to someone professional about what she was experiencing. She also hoped that this would help to repair the marriage and to deal with her sense of anger, confusion and shame. She spoke to a friend, who was able to put her in touch with a therapist.

Distress can also be a problem on its own. For example, certain chemical changes or imbalances within the body can produce feelings of distress. It is important that we are aware of our feelings and, in particular, feelings that may cause significant distress, either in relation to some circumstances that we are struggling with or because our bodies are reacting within a situation. Grief from loss can be one of the most powerful and unsettling feelings that we experience. Some people find that the feelings get worse before they start to feel better, as Harriet discovered.

Harriet's mother died from cancer six months before Harriet sought psychological counselling. At the time of her mother's death, she felt numb in herself and explained that she felt she was in a cloud and 'on automatic'. She was supported by friends and family, and the fact that she had expected her mother's death meant that when it came it was perhaps slightly less of a shock. However, in the months that passed she experienced the full intensity of the loss and felt lonely in herself. The feelings were uncomfortable to the point of being unbearable, and yet she did not feel she wanted to talk to friends and family about what she was experiencing because she did not want to be a burden to them.

> Finally, she could bear the pain no more and plucked up the courage to phone a bereavement counselling service, who responded to her difficulties in a professional and compassionate way.

Events in most people's lives can be unpredictable. As we progress through life from childhood to adolescence, young adulthood, adulthood and to the older adult, we are confronted with new challenges and experiences which may lead to us experiencing new and sometimes difficult feelings. The good news is that most people overcome difficulties in their lives and cope with experiences, even if they have had to make big changes in order for this to happen. Therapy should not be, nor need be, a first resort for dealing with life's difficulties. Sometimes, therapy can be overplayed a little and the idea that we need to seek therapy whenever we experience difficulties in our lives is something that most therapists would be hesitant to believe. At times, however, even the most resourceful and robust among us can feel vulnerable or overwhelmed when faced by some unexpected or seemingly impossible challenge, trauma or circumstance, or simply having too many things to deal with at the same time. Therapy may help at such times.

Therapy in our time: having no-one else to talk to

If your personal circumstances change rapidly, it may be that stress you would normally cope well with may become too much for you to manage. With migration of workers to large urban settings, it is now common for a person to be separated for extended periods of time from many normal human supports such as family, friends and a familiar language and culture. There may be no-one else who is close at hand with whom it is possible to share what might be considered normal daily stress or hassle. In such circumstances it is becoming increasingly commonplace for people to seek the help of a professional for support in what may feel like an overwhelming, confusing and lonely environment.

If you happen to be such a person, cut off from your home culture, deprived of the normal daily support of family and friends and beginning to feel low without being able to shake this feeling off, it may be worth considering talking through your situation with a therapist. Therapists are trained to help you improve your ability to cope at such times. Fatema was just such an individual who was able to benefit from her contact with a university counsellor.

> Fatema, a 24-year-old from West Africa, had remained in her room at a students' residence of a large city university for the first four weeks of her master's degree programme without meeting anyone or attending lectures. She was then discovered by the warden of the residence, who subsequently arranged a meeting for her with the university counsellor. Fatema told the counsellor that prior to coming to university she had never even gone unaccompanied to her local village shop. She said she had felt lost and frightened ever since she arrived in the city. Having the opportunity to talk through her problems with the counsellor helped Fatema to get back on track with her life.

Another feature of modern life that characterizes the Western world is the constant stimulation and distraction that we all now experience through the continuous bombardment of the senses via e-communication. The information explosion at best can inform, enliven and enrich, but at worst it can deplete, overwhelm and overextend people, depriving them of regular human interaction. It has become common now for many people to spend long hours each day in front of a computer screen. Contact with colleagues and friends is often replaced by text and email, to the exclusion of face-to-face interaction. Such isolation experienced over a sustained period of time can lead to the burgeoning of common psychological problems, which is precisely what happened with 33-year-old Reeve.

> A new job had brought Reeve to the big city for the first time. He now lived at a considerable distance from his family and friends, and visits back there were costly. Soon after arriving in his new location, Reeve had begun a relationship with a woman. Eighteen months later he was made redundant, and at the same time his relationship broke up. Reeve then decided to start up his own IT business from his small flat. This required him to spend many hours each day working on his computer. Sociable and friendly by nature, he began to feel more and more lonely and vulnerable and soon was going out only when it was absolutely

essential. As he began to feel low, his change of mood was picked up by his observant GP at a routine medical check and he was referred by the GP for therapy. Through discussions with the therapist, Reeve's mood gradually started to improve. He slowly began to regain his self-confidence so that he began again to enjoy a social life and restore some life–work balance in his life.

Conclusion

Although in this chapter we have attempted to cover the main issues that frequently prompt people to see a therapist, people find their way to psychological therapy via a number of different routes, as can be seen from the above cases. Some feel that they have an identifiable and specific problem which they want to work on. Others encounter feelings that they are finding difficult to understand or cope with. For others still, it may be a desire to explore personal issues, whether these are to do with relationships or other patterns in their life that may prompt them to request psychological therapy. Circumstances and the presence or absence of a support network impacts on a person's ability to cope.

It is worth pointing out that none of the problems or issues named in this chapter can *only* be discussed with a therapist! Research suggests that many of the different activities, discussions, behaviours, interactions and conversations that we have with different people in our lives in a great variety of settings can be 'therapeutic'. Other chapters in this book will elaborate more on these ideas. Chapter 6 highlights many suggestions about what you can do yourself to improve your mental health and well-being and the changes you can make to help you get the most out of therapy or, for some, make seeing a therapist unnecessary.

4

Main approaches of therapy

Would you prefer a therapist who talks and interacts with you as in any other conversation (the only difference is that the focus of the conversation is on you!) or a therapist who lets you do most of the talking? The manner of the therapist and the way she may interact with you will reflect the different approaches of therapy. You may be unfamiliar with some or any of the main 'brand' names or therapy schools followed by therapists. Don't be concerned if you feel that you have only limited or even no knowledge or understanding of some of these. It would be a tall order to expect anyone seeking therapy to be aware of the differences between them and the possible advantages of one over the other.

Most people have, however, heard of Sigmund Freud as he is regarded as the founder and 'father' of therapy. His ideas have continued to have influence, and even today some of the ideas and techniques that he developed are in use. He developed an important theory about 'unconscious processes' which are those drives, instincts, feelings or actions that influence how we relate, but about which we may not have any or complete awareness. He remains a well-recognized figure in both therapy and popular culture, and cartoons depicting therapy often represent the therapist as a Freud-like, bearded man seated at the head of a couch with a note pad on his lap. His approach is termed 'psychodynamic'.

Few therapists adopt a purely Freudian approach even though some of the ideas from this approach may be introduced in your therapy sessions. Many therapy approaches have at their core the supportive and professional relationship between client and therapist in which the client's needs and concerns are the focus. Almost all approaches nowadays are client-centred, which means that *your* issues or problems will be addressed. This also means that the therapy process will respect your individual needs, such as which issues get dealt with first and also perhaps the pace at which therapy progresses. Most approaches will actively involve you in the process, such as with Nicola, whose counsellor in the student counselling service used cognitive behaviour therapy.

Nicola, aged 19, was coming to the end of her first year of study at university and had occasionally used recreational drugs. Fortunately, she had stopped after several experiences because she found it an unpleasant experience. However, she felt overwhelmed by exam stress and had in the back of her mind that maybe some of her drug-using experiences had affected her anxiety and confidence. She felt she could not concentrate and prepare for exams, which in turn made her more agitated and worried about her performance at university. Nicola became increasingly desperate and the symptoms of her anxiety became more apparent to her. She would start retching when she woke up in the morning and felt that her mind would not focus on work. She sought the help of the university counselling service for her exam anxiety and for coping with general stress. The counsellor was friendly and seemed genuinely interested in Nicola's experience and anxiety problem. She explained that, with exams only three weeks away, she would help Nicola to understand how anxiety symptoms develop and how and what Nicola could do to try to overcome them. She told Nicola that the approach she used, called cognitive behaviour therapy, examines how our thoughts about situations and behaviours or reactions can trigger anxiety and panic attacks. This in turn, she said, was also the key to overcoming the problem. She provided Nicola with some exercises she could try out which would reduce her anxiety and help her to regain her confidence for her exams.

Therapy involves talking about some personal and sensitive issues, and it is only natural that your therapist should work with you in an empathic way and strive to respect your feelings and personal experiences. After all, it is easier to open up to someone who engages positively and actively with you when you feel emotionally distressed and who tries to understand what you are going through, than to someone who may seem aloof or distant. Some clients are comfortable doing most of the work, such as talking and bringing material to sessions. Others may prefer a more guided or focused approach. Neither is better than the other, but your personal needs and taste should play a part in your choice of therapist or approach, if these are important to you. This was something that Renée briefly thought about before she was referred for client-centred therapy.

Renée felt very uneasy in herself a year on from being held up and kept hostage in a bank raid. At first, Renée was understandably shocked and distressed by the very unpleasant event. However, through support provided by the bank and good family backing, she gradually felt better in herself and was able to return to work. However, it was while watching the news one night that she felt uneasy in herself when one of the local news items was about a bank raid. She suddenly felt as if she was experiencing the whole episode again. It also coincided with the one-year anniversary of the event. She started having flashbacks to the event and could not erase the picture of the masked man holding a revolver standing threateningly in front of her. She started to shake uncontrollably and felt that she was losing control of herself. Recognizing the link between what she was experiencing and the bank raid a year ago, she wondered whether she had been experiencing post-traumatic stress symptoms. She remembered that she had the contact details of a counselling service that was made available to her at the time of the bank raid. She contacted them and they offered to see her within a day. She was glad that she had been given an appointment so soon but then started to worry about what she would say, how she might come across to the therapist and whether she would have to talk about her past and her childhood. The telephone counsellor who arranged her face-to-face session for the next day reassured Renée that the therapist she was seeing would first invite her to talk about her experience of the bank raid in her own time, and that she did not need to worry about talking about her childhood if she didn't want to. The telephone counsellor said that the therapist worked in a client-centred way, and that she would work to try to gain a clear understanding of what Renée had been through so that she would feel supported in a trusting relationship.

If you take a look at Table 4.1, you will find a brief outline of three main therapeutic approaches commonly used in the UK which we have briefly touched on above. These are psychodynamic therapy, client-centred therapy and cognitive behaviour therapy. Rather than list and address the couple of hundred other different theoretical approaches in this compact book – which would be an impossible task – we have chosen instead to emphasize these three main approaches as most therapists will be familiar with them and are likely to draw on most or all of the key aspects of the approach. This will help you when you contact a therapist or meet for a first session, so that you can have a clearer idea of how things might develop in sessions and what you can expect to be the main focus.

Table 4.1 The three main therapeutic approaches

What's it called?	What's the thinking behind it?	What happens in therapy?
Person-centred therapy Also 'client-centred' or 'humanistic' therapy	Everyone is unique but we all have the capacity to grow towards being the best person we can possibly be. This is most likely to happen when we feel understood and valued by others and becomes more difficult if we encounter rejection or hostility. Because our experiences are unique to each one of us, our view of ourselves, others and the world about us will also be unique. Therefore, we all think about and react to similar situations in different ways. This means that you are the expert on why you might be distressed or why you find situations difficult which others seem to cope with. By providing an environment where you are unconditionally valued and understood, the aim is to allow you to explore whatever has brought you to therapy and use your own knowledge and skills to find ways of living in the best way for you. People often describe this sort of therapy as having a companion who values and understands them, without judging, on a journey towards being the best person they can be – often referred	Your therapist will encourage you to tell your story at your own pace. Initially you will probably focus together on whatever has brought you to therapy. Together you might then decide that some of your earlier experiences, perhaps from childhood, are important to help you both understand what is happening now. When this is the case, you will explore those together as well. As you work with your therapist, she will probably summarize what you have talked about fairly frequently. This is to check that you both understand what has been said and to check with you, as the expert on your situation, on the meaning of what has been said. You will probably find that you are often encouraged to consider how you feel about situations or people you talk about and the impact they have had on you. This is one way of helping you to identify your way of thinking and the skills and knowledge you have. Your therapist is unlikely to answer questions such as 'What should I do about this?' This is because you are the person most likely to find

Table 4.1 Contd.

What's it called?	What's the thinking behind it?	What happens in therapy?
	to as 'personal growth'. They often say that spending time with a therapist who provides this experience also shows them what it can be like to interact with other people in ways which are most likely to be positive experiences for everyone involved.	the best answer. The therapist will help you find a way to answer these questions yourself, because you're the expert on your experience and situation. Therapy is not a passive process. Sometimes you may find it quite demanding! Sessions are normally once a week, with some flexibility. Most commonly six to ten sessions but can also be long term.
Cognitive behaviour therapy Also 'CBT', 'cognitive therapy'	What we think and what we do both affect what we feel emotionally and physically. For example, • If I pass a friend in the street and he ignores me, I might think that he was annoyed with me. I'd probably feel upset or worried. If I thought he had forgotten his glasses and couldn't see me, I might feel sorry for him or even amused. So what I think can affect how I feel. • If I avoid going to the dentist because I think it will be painful or frightening, I might not find out that often that's not true, and I will probably remain anxious. What I do has affected how I think and what I feel. By working with ways of thinking and acting that aren't helpful, the aim is to change how you feel. It's also often important to look at what we do to try and make our situation better – like	Your therapist will help you to look for the ways you think and the things you do that aren't helpful to you. You will then work together on adapting some of what you think and do and see what effect that has on how you feel. Working with what you think might involve keeping a note of unhelpful thoughts and checking how those thoughts make you feel. When thoughts aren't helpful, your therapist will work with you to find a new way of thinking based on genuine facts which you can test out yourself, or to decide what you could do to manage the situation that is making you think that way. Working with what you do might involve safely trying out new ways of doing things, making changes at a pace that's manageable for you.

Table 4.1 Contd.

What's it called?	What's the thinking behind it?	What happens in therapy?
	avoiding the dentist. Sometimes these 'safety behaviours' stop us finding better ways to cope or even mean we aren't as well or as happy as we could be. Avoiding the dentist, for example, could mean I'm more likely to have bad teeth! This therapy is often thought of as teaching skills to cope with difficult situations and unhelpful ways of thinking or acting. People often talk about using what they have been taught when they meet challenges or find things difficult well after therapy has finished. Some even say they have been trained to be their own 'therapist' if they encounter similar difficulties in the future. This can make you more confident in your ability to cope.	The aim is to teach you the skills to do this for yourself, and some work often needs to be done between sessions. Your therapist will help you identify what's worked well and what can be learnt from trying out new ways of thinking and doing. Sessions are normally once a week but can be more flexible. Usually six to ten sessions but can sometimes be long term.
Psychodynamic therapy	We have two ways of thinking: conscious or 'surface-level' thoughts which we can easily describe and are always aware of, and unconscious or subconscious 'hidden' thoughts which are more difficult to identify. Unconscious thinking is probably the result of our early experiences, particularly as infants, and it can be supportive or unhelpful. The way in which we behave is driven by our unconscious thoughts, particularly by the desire to be safe. For example:	You might be invited to lie on a couch similar to the ones you may have seen in television dramas or newspaper cartoons, but you're more likely to talk to your therapist face to face, seated in a chair. Many psychodynamic therapists will spend some time focusing with you on your early experiences and childhood. Generally, your therapist won't say very much but will encourage you to say whatever comes into your mind. This means that if you're not feeling very talkative some sessions can be very quiet.

Table 4.1 Contd.

What's it called?	What's the thinking behind it?	What happens in therapy?
	• If as a child I was encouraged to interact with other people and usually discovered that they were enjoyable to be with, I'd probably have learnt to unconsciously think about people as interesting and fun and I'd be likely to be sociable and interact with many people as an adult. By paying close attention to the moods, feelings and underlying messages in what you talk about, the aim is to become aware of your unconscious thoughts. One of the main ways therapists do this is by being aware of their own reactions to you. A large part of their training is long-term therapy to identify their own unconscious thoughts. This means that they can identify the part of their reaction to you which is a reflection of your unconscious thoughts and use this to help you identify them. This might sound strange, but you could think of your therapist as using her own experience to be particularly sensitive to your thoughts and feelings. This type of therapy is sometimes described as using your therapist as a way of reflecting your thoughts back to you so that you can start to become more aware of unconscious thoughts and feelings.	Long silences will not worry your therapist although they may be uncomfortable for you, especially at first. You may find long pauses useful to reflect on what you have been talking about or how you feel. Occasionally, your therapist may suggest an interpretation of what you have said or ask you to pay attention to something you are thinking. Psychodynamic therapists will almost never answer questions like 'Where are you going on holiday?' or 'Are you working late today?' This is because their aim is to keep their own personality out of the work they are doing with you so that they can truly reflect what you are thinking or feeling. They will probably respond by asking you to explore why you might need to know. Psychodynamic therapy is often intense, with up to three sessions per week for long periods of time, although there are some forms which use six to ten weekly sessions. Psychoanalysis may take place over months or years.

Perhaps even more important in therapy than the 'brand name' used, from your point of view, is whether your individual needs are met in therapy sessions. Where this happens, you feel a good 'fit' between you and your therapist. The reason we emphasize the importance of 'fit' in therapy is that the relationship that develops between you and your therapist, and how you feel about the way you are getting along in your sessions, is vital. Put another way, if you feel that you are in a supportive and helpful relationship with your therapist, you may enjoy greater progress in your sessions with her.

Below is a summary of what clients often state is most important to them in therapy sessions. These are core to the therapeutic experience irrespective of the model or professional background of their therapist.

- Your needs are put first.
- You feel listened to and understood.
- You do not feel judged.
- You feel that you are in the presence of somebody who is experienced, professional and principled.
- You feel that your therapist conveys warmth, support, care and empathy.
- You feel clear about the practical aspects of therapy (such as the contract).
- It is agreed and understood that everything said in sessions is kept confidential.
- Your therapist explains how she can (or cannot) help with your issues.
- You feel some optimism or hope about coping with or overcoming your issues.

We cannot describe or prescribe which therapy approaches work best for specific psychological problems. There is value and merit – and limitations – in all of the approaches used. Currently, there is scientific evidence to suggest that cognitive behavioural therapy (CBT) can be helpful in the treatment of common psychological problems such as depression and anxiety. The skill of the therapist is, however, still important in the success of therapy. The most important outcome in therapy is whether you feel your needs have been met and issues addressed. That is why we have highlighted the most important of these in the list above, which can help you to determine from an early stage whether you feel that a good working relationship can develop.

You may find it helpful to have a first session with a therapist to determine whether you feel comfortable working with her. This is an opportunity for you to assess whether you want to carry on with her and within the style and approach that she uses. There is often no short cut to choosing a therapist other than to meet with a possible individual. After all, it would be unlikely that you would buy a car based on reading a brochure alone: at some point you would want to test-drive the car. The same applies to therapy. You can learn about a therapist's credentials or reputation through a website or personal recommendation. She may have many letters after her name attesting to her qualifications. But at the end of the day, as with most personal relationships, you will need to experience it at first hand. Hopefully, things will work well for you. If they don't, it is not wrong to end the therapy and try someone else. Trust your instinct!

5

Choosing a therapist or counsellor

You've decided that you might want to talk to a therapist about whether therapy is a useful way forward for you; the next step is choosing someone to visit. This can feel almost overwhelming initially, particularly if you are already worried about other things. So we are breaking this chapter into several sections to help you make your choice. Remember the old saying, 'The only way to eat an elephant is one bite at a time.'

From the start, it is important to rid yourself of the idea that people who see a therapist are 'mad', mentally ill or weak. The vast majority of people visiting a therapist are like you and me – 'the worried well'. This means that at this moment, they have a concern, a crisis, a situation that they are finding it difficult to resolve or live with. It may have lasted a few weeks, a few months or a few days.

Why?

First of all, think about why you want to see a counsellor.

- You may already have tried a number of other things to resolve your issue. We talk more about these in Chapter 6, but they may have included talking to friends and family, consulting your GP, reflexology, aromatherapy or other complementary therapies, or simply trying to distract yourself by busying yourself with work and social events. All of these things can be useful, but if they are not working you may decide to see a therapist.
- It could be that you want to talk to someone independent and neutral. Friends, family and work colleagues all know you and have a particular view on what you should do. With the best will in the world, people you know are generally

biased and may have preformed opinions about the situation or about other people involved in it. A counsellor will listen non-judgementally, and will work with you to find ways forward that reflect your needs and wishes. She is not there to tell you what to do or usually to give you advice.

- It is generally better to decide to do something about the situation sooner rather than later. It's a bit like having a physical problem; your GP would rather see you earlier on than when the problem has become more serious. That doesn't mean that we are suggesting you should see a therapist for every little problem. Many things we worry about are quite common and often very normal things that many other people worry about, so we can resolve them ourselves. However, many of us do try to battle our way through problems, feeling that we 'should be able to sort them out ourselves'. But that is not always possible and we find ourselves going round in circles. This is where a therapist may be able to help us.

How?

The next question is likely to be: how do I find a therapist? It can seem very challenging as you may not be feeling at your best, but hang on to your common sense and be prepared to use your gut instinct about who is right for you.

- You could talk to your GP. Some surgeries have a therapist as part of their practice team. If not, they may be able to refer you to someone. If the counsellor is attached the practice, then this is usually a free service. However, if the GP refers you or gives you a list of local therapists in your area, you may have to pay.
- You could look in the Yellow Pages, or Thomson Directories. Counsellors and therapists are usually found in the 'Counselling and Advice' sections, but be aware that there may also be people who deal with other things such as debt listed in those sections, so check whether they are therapeutic counsellors if you contact them.

- Search the internet. Remember that if you just google 'counsellors' you will come up with a list running into thousands! You need to refine the search to something like 'counsellors in West Sussex' or 'counsellors in Winchester'. Even then, the list may be daunting.
- If doing an internet search throws up too many people for you to decide between, a better way might be to look on specific websites of organizations such as the British Association for Counselling and Psychotherapy (BACP), the United Kingdom Council for Psychotherapy (UKCP), the British Psychological Society (BPS) or the British Association for Behavioural and Cognitive Psychotherapies (BABCP). These websites include an area-by-area directory of professionally trained counsellors. Consulting the lists of professional bodies like these gives you some safety, as therapists' qualifications will have been checked and they will have the necessary professional insurance.
- If you have friends or acquaintances who have been in therapy, they may be able to tell you about local people. It's important to realize, though, that just because a therapist suited one person does not mean she will suit you, so talk to the therapist first before committing yourself.

What?

So, what happens in therapy? Most people work with a trained counsellor or psychotherapist in a *one-to-one* setting. It might be with someone in:

- independent practice;
- a counselling organization;
- a health or hospital setting.

It is also possible to go with your partner and engage in *couples counselling*. The best-known providers of couples work are probably Relate and Marriage Care. However, many independent practitioners also work with couples, though when you contact them it is a good idea to check out whether they are trained or experienced in providing this type of therapy.

More difficult to access is *family therapy*, where all or most of the family members go together to look at issues affecting the lives of everyone in that family system. There are fewer trained family therapists than individual or couple counsellors, so if this is what you are looking for, it is probably best to ask your GP for help in finding one. Sadly, there may well be quite a long waiting list for this type of support.

Therapy is also offered in *groups*. These are often for clients who are all interested in resolving the same or a similar issue in their lives. Like family therapy, it may be difficult to find and access these except through the NHS. This type of therapy can be extremely effective, as you have the benefit of hearing about other people's experience and solutions, which may help you make your own choices and resolutions.

Therapy does not have to take place only face to face, though this is by far the most common way at present. It can happen by using the *telephone* or the *internet*. These methods are particularly useful for people who are housebound through disability or through carer roles. It is also a helpful way of engaging in therapeutic work for those living in rural or isolated areas, or where there is limited public transport, if they do not have their own car. There is more about online work in Chapter 8.

There are many very good telephone helplines and websites that specialize in particular areas such as bereavement, eating disorders and addiction issues (see Useful addresses for details). They may be able to signpost you to practitioners in your area if you need more than they can offer.

You may wish to contact a *specialist agency*. These focus, like the helplines and websites we've mentioned, on specific issues. Cruse is a well-known one for bereavement, and there are counselling organizations for young people between 11 and 25 in most major towns and cities. Because they often offer free or low-cost contracts, there may be a waiting list to see someone.

For some people, counselling is available through their *workplace*. Some larger companies and public service organizations have their own in-house counselling service. These can be accessed either through self-referral or through occupational health or human resources departments. Other companies buy in external providers to offer counselling to employees, and sometimes to their families. These are usually called employee assistance programmes (EAPs). If they are available, they enable employees to undertake short-term counselling with an external, independent counsellor. The number of sessions available is mostly between four and eight, depending on the agreement between your employer and the EAP. There is often information about these internal and external provisions in your pay slip envelope. Some people worry about whether their boss will know about the counselling and issues discussed, but these are confidential services. These company-provided schemes are obviously free, so it is worth investigating whether your workplace offers one.

How much?

The cost of therapy is an important factor. The person who charges the highest fee is not necessarily the best or most experienced, nor is the person charging the lowest the worst and least trained! Do ask about fees very early in a conversation about whether you can work with this therapist. This is a business arrangement, as well as one to help you resolve concerns, so practitioners are used to people asking about fees.

Fees depend on a number of factors.

- Geographical location – in London and other large cities, overheads are likely to be higher, and the fee will reflect this.
- Someone working from her own home does not have to pay rent, so this may account for some differences.
- A recently qualified practitioner may charge less than a very experienced one – that doesn't necessarily mean that she won't provide a good service!
- If you want appointments at unsocial hours (early mornings, later in the evening or at weekends) you may find you pay a higher fee.
- Some practitioners offer a slight discount if you pay for several sessions up front.

- Others will reduce the fees after a number of sessions if you decide you want longer-term work.

Don't be afraid to ask if there is a sliding scale of charges. Some therapists have a scheme whereby their charges are based on the client's income. This is quite rare, but what is a little more common is for therapists to reserve a few appointments that they are prepared to offer at a lower fee to low or unwaged clients, or those on benefit allowances. Obviously these get filled quickly, so clients may have to wait for an available slot before beginning therapy.

When you initially contact someone, do ask what the charge is for an initial appointment. This can vary considerably. Occasionally, therapists offer a free session or a reduced fee for such an appointment, while others may charge more as they are making an assessment of the client's needs. As you may want to visit two or three practitioners to decide who you feel you can best work with, it is important to ask these questions!

Who?

This last point about seeing a couple of counsellors for initial appointments brings us to the question of who you choose. This is such an individual thing, and there are no right or easy answers. However, consider which of the points below are important to you. We have listed them from the general through to the specific.

- How far away from your home (or your work) is the therapist located? It is really the time taken to get there which matters, not the actual mileage. If it takes more than 30 minutes either way, is it too far? Remember, sessions are usually around 50 minutes to an hour, so that will be two hours altogether out of your day.
- Do you need to use public transport, and if so, how reliable and frequent are the services to the therapist's location?
- Do you want to work with a man or a woman?

- Do you want someone 'like you' – for example, someone from the same culture, the same age group, the same economic or social group – or do you want someone who is different from you? Or does this not matter to you?
- How easy was it to be in contact with the therapist initially? (Most therapists are not available to talk to you when you phone as they are with clients, but did she phone you back reasonably soon, or were you left wondering whether she ever would get back to you?)
- When you first met her, did she seem welcoming?
- Was she prepared to talk about practical things like money, length of sessions, whether you can contact her between sessions, and what happens if you cannot make an appointment?
- Did she tell you about her qualifications and training if you asked? And which professional bodies she belongs to?
- Could she explain her approach to you? (There is more about different approaches in Chapter 4; you might want to read this first, so that you know a bit more about what is on offer and what might suit you.)
- Was she prepared to answer questions about her professional experience, such as 'How long have you been practising?' or 'Have you worked with issues like this before?' or 'When might confidentiality be broken?'
- If you decide to work with her, will you go on the same day, at the same time, every week? This may suit you very well, with your other commitments. However, if you need more flexibility, is this possible for the therapist as well, with her own commitments?
- Will she discuss how long the process might last and how it ends? (No therapist can predict exactly the number of sessions you will need, but she should be prepared to talk to you about how you would both recognize what is working and when the counselling is coming to an end.)
- Under what circumstances might she decide that she wants to refer you to another professional?

- Does this person feel 'right' for you? For example, do you feel that you will be able to talk to her? This is possibly a gut feeling, but it is usually worth trusting yourself in this matter.
- Remember that you have the right to stop at any time if it is not working for you. Although it may seem an odd thing to discuss before you even start to work with someone, it is a good idea to ask what happens if you decide to end because it is not helping you. It is easier to do this when it's hypothetical than if it is a reality. If you don't like the answer, then don't work with that person.

Conclusion

Just to sum up this chapter, it is crucial that you choose the right person for you. You want to talk to your counsellor about matters that are of huge importance to you, and you need to be able to trust him or her. You wouldn't buy a major item for the house without thinking about what you wanted or needed, what you like and dislike, so don't just pull a name out of a telephone directory and feel you have to settle for that person! You are the client, and your life and your issues are not to be treated lightly.

6

Practical steps you can take to help yourself, or how to chew an elephant

Research confirms that the pathways to sound mental health and well-being are now well signposted. This signposting is for the most part a rather straightforward, even pedestrian business. No complex theory of human behaviour is needed to achieve this objective. Many of us, indeed most of us, will feel stressed out, sad, miserable or depressed at some time in our lives. This chapter outlines certain changes you can begin to make by yourself, that are proven to be helpful in enhancing or restoring your general health and well-being. For some, such steps may be enough in themselves. For others, the need to seek professional help may be further highlighted. The practical changes outlined here could also augment and supplement any formal therapeutic process you may have embarked upon and arguably should be encouraged before any formal therapy begins.

Even small steps taken in some or any of the following suggested pathways can contribute significantly to improved physical and mental health. Taking the first steps in such directions can be as important as getting on to the right motorway in the direction of any desired destination. If you are already engaged with some of these practices – do more of them! Good luck!

Feeling low

Depression or feeling low is one of the commonest psychological problems. Depression can undermine our confidence and sense of well-being. It can deprive us of joy and can deplete our lives of meaning. Depression can impact on every aspect of our lives, as it did Scott's.

Scott was a 33-year-old media consultant who came to see his GP three years after the traumatic break-up of a long-term relationship with his girlfriend. He said that he had been having difficulties in sleeping during the prior three years and that recently he had not been able to sleep at all. Scott also said that for three years he had only eaten junk food and had put on several kilos in weight. He said he had begun to feel very tearful recently. He no longer enjoyed anything and he admitted that for the last two weeks he had been unable to get himself to work. He had come to see the GP because during the previous night he had felt so scared and agitated that he had been unable to stay on his own. He had gone to a friend's flat during the night asking for shelter. Scott's friend had persuaded him to go and see his GP the following day. During questioning by the GP it emerged that Scott had been working a punishing schedule for the last three years from 5.00 a.m. to 12.00 p.m. seven days a week. He had not taken any days off during that time. He had lost his connection with almost all his friends. He did not have a partner and had lost contact with his family. Scott said he felt 'terrible' and he was unable to figure out how this had happened. The worst aspect of it all was the fact that he could not sleep.

Many people, like Scott, present themselves to their GP with one or more physical symptoms or complaints when they are depressed. Most people who are depressed experience negative thinking. This fact is understood by psychologists to be the crucial factor in depression, yet many people fail to recognize this aspect of their experience as part of depression. When we are depressed, our thoughts tend to be negative. This negative bias in our thinking is not always an accurate reflection of reality but we can be very convinced by our thoughts.

Later on in this chapter we will return to the central role negative thinking plays in contributing to maintaining our low, sad or anxious feelings. What *is* helpful to consider briefly at this point is the following well-established fact in relation to negative thinking. A characteristic of our negative thought pattern is that it is often experienced by the individual as relentless, compelling and at times compulsive. If we are feeling upset or distressed because we have lost a job or failed an exam or suffered an insult, we can get sucked into our thinking. There is often no time limit to this practice. We can keep doing it, so that we could be described as almost living in our brain. It is often the very bright, most resourceful and able among us who persist longer in this activity in the attempt to solve our particular problem. However, the more we try, the worse we feel. Our best efforts bring no solution. Indeed, our situation frequently worsens!

To help illustrate this point, recall a time when you had something on your mind that so worried you that you might not have noticed the street you were walking on, or maybe your car seemed to find its own way home without you driving it although you did sit at the wheel. We call this functioning on autopilot. When depression gets entrenched, people can become more and more focused on what is going on in their brain and less and less on what is going on around them.

> Ilaria, a highly intelligent but depressed 22-year-old woman, vividly described to her therapist an experience she had at work. She had been asked to complete a work task in front of her line manger and her supervisor. She was aware that if she performed well it could contribute to promotion for her. Ilaria recounted the fact that at the time, although she was very aware of the importance of her performance at the assigned task, she recalled having to constantly struggle not to get engaged with what her brain was trying to focus on! Her thoughts were repeatedly going over and over the reasons her relationship had broken up, which had led to her current low mood. Ilaria described how she had to fight the impulse to run out of the room away from her work colleagues so that she could 'be with her thoughts'.

Ilaria's experience, although apparently extreme, is not uncommon when people are depressed. Ilaria resisted the urge to flee from the room and the presence of her supervisor. Think for a moment of the possible scenario if she had given in to the pull of her negative thoughts and had left the room or, worse still, avoided coming to work entirely. Avoidance and withdrawal behaviour are often a characteristic of low mood.

When our thoughts are negative, our behaviours – the things we do and the things we do not do – can often make matters worse. One of the consequences, when our mood is low, of getting more and more caught up in our negative thought process is that we can cut out of our lives many life-giving and relaxing activities such as leisure pursuits, hobbies, interests and physical exercise. Our life–work balance gets lost and social and personal relationships get forgotten or ignored. Concentration and motivation become impaired so that our ability to think in productive and life-enhancing ways diminishes. Even getting through the day may become a struggle. Learning new skills becomes impossible. This process can be imagined as a funnel shape pointing downwards. As our low mood intensifies, more and more of our attention gets directed towards our thoughts. Neglect of ordinary physical needs such as eating and sleeping can occur. In advanced cases, even basic hygiene can be forgotten and ignored.

The problem can seem to take on the dimensions of an elephant as the situation can feel so overwhelming. The question may then arise: how does one go about chewing an elephant? As we found out in Chapter 5, the answer is 'in bite-sized pieces'. A good beginning, then, is to try to reinstate some of those activities, behaviours and hobbies that we have almost unknowingly excised from our lives in small and manageable 'bite-sized' pieces.

A word of caution here: if you are experiencing symptoms to the degree that you are currently engaged in any kind of self-harming behaviour or have thoughts about ending your life, it is crucial that you 'break' self-imposed silence and urgently seek professional help from a medical or trained professional. You do not have to go on enduring such misery alone.

Even though the theme of this book is encouraging the idea of seeking professional help when things are difficult, remember that when someone's mood is low, as Scott's was, it may be very difficult to take any action at all. Usually we wait to want to do things. When depressed we rarely 'want' to do anything! Even routine daily chores as simple as drawing back the curtains, buying a newspaper, keeping a date with a friend, can become almost impossible tasks to accomplish. At the beginning of this process of making small changes, do not have the expectation that you will feel better immediately. It is a question of doing and knowing that you are on the correct pathway. Feeling better comes later.

Although an order has been imposed on the suggestions below for the sake of clarity, any one of them can be a useful starting point. Depression is different for everyone, so it is important to begin to do what appeals to you most or what feels most possible.

Recognizing the difficulty

Acknowledge the problem

To identify the fact that there is a problem is a crucial first step to take. Reading this book may help you to recognize some of the signs of low mood or other psychological difficulties. Acknowledging that there is a problem is not always easy. When we feel sad, low or stressed out we can also feel self-critical, incompetent and frustrated by our own inability to improve the situation. We can then 'bury' negative feelings and emotional difficulties. This can make things worse however, as it did for Scott. His situation became so serious that he could no longer function. Scott was unable to see that he had a problem until his friend pointed it out to him. This is not uncommon.

Talking can help

Breaking the silence that frequently accompanies the process of feeling stressed or depressed is a good thing. This is often a very difficult decision to take. It is important to choose wisely the person in whom you wish to confide, whether this is a friend, colleague or professional. If one is responded to with warmth, understanding and without any criticism it is usually very helpful. Some people deliberately choose not to confide in anyone close to them as they do not wish the other to be upset or burdened by their problem. Others fear that any disclosure of personal distress or difficulty may be equated with weakness, incompetence or failure. Some may feel they run the risk of being critically appraised or judged and may 'lose face' if they state how they feel. Even worse, some can feel that their professional role might be jeopardized if any expression of what may be construed as personal weakness or vulnerability is expressed.

If you are in this situation and for any reason find yourself without a confidante, it may be that it is appropriate to think about consulting a professional – either a GP, a nurse practitioner or a therapist. Before embarking on this course there may be other steps you can take that may contribute to your feeling better and minimize the need to seek out professional help, so read on!

Looking after your body

Improve sleep habits

A sound night's sleep is universally prized. Interrupted or disturbed sleep causes great distress and can also be a common sign of psychological distress, as in the case of Scott. Disturbed sleep continues to be the focus of much research and reflection on the part of scientists and psychological experts. If you are suffering interrupted sleep, the distilled essence of modern research in helping you to redress this situation in a practical and pragmatic way is contained in Chapter 10 of this book. We urge you to read it now. All of the following steps described hereafter, if implemented, may also contribute to sound sleep.

Establish a pattern of regular exercise

The human body is designed to move. Not moving or moving little is not conducive to a healthy body or mind. Establishing a pattern of regular physical exercise is the single most useful stress redresser there is. Sometimes low mood may be accompanied by restlessness and agitation. More often, when people are depressed they find that to engage with any activity, however little, can be difficult. When re-engaging with any physical exercise it is therefore important to set small and manageable goals for yourself at first and then to gradually build up to more extended periods of exercise.

Activity impacts on body chemistry which in turn contributes to emotional well-being. If you begin to take note of your mood before and following any session of exercise, invariably there will be a perceptible improvement in your mood. To begin to re-engage with physical activity or to start for the first time, some kind of regular exercise can be the first step in beginning to regain some sense of taking control back in your life and the start of feeling better. Remember, then – physical exercise is not optional in the restoration or maintenance of emotional well-being. If you suffer from a medical condition it is better to first discuss with your GP the amount of physical exercise that is right for you. The benefits of exercise and suggestions about how you might begin an exercise programme are described in Chapter 10. We suggest that you read that now before proceeding further with this chapter.

Healthy eating

What we eat impacts on our mood. This is now a well-established scientific fact. You can help to boost, restore and maintain physical and psychological well-being by eating healthily. A few helpful rules to keep in mind might be: eat only when you are hungry; cut out eating junk food; eat every food in moderation and eat a variety of foods; eat three small meals a day instead of one very large one, and no snacking in between! Chapter 10 of this book contains a section on how to improve your eating. We recommend that you read it.

Restoring pleasure, developing resilience and competence

Participate in activities that you enjoy

The inability to take pleasure or experience a sense of delight or joy in any aspect of life is a common experience when depressed. It is therefore important to begin to re-engage with an activity, leisure pursuit or hobby that you once enjoyed (or always thought that you might enjoy) even if it is as simple as walking your dog, playing your favourite sport, spending time with a friend, taking a lunch break, writing a letter or email to a loved one. It may be necessary to give yourself permission to do this as life can seem a serious business indeed when you feel low! Do not expect to be able to enjoy any such activity straight away. This is really important to keep in mind. The initial objective is to engage with the activity – not to expect to get pleasure from it immediately. Pleasure may take some time to return.

An alternative starting point could be to begin noticing in your daily life any behaviours or activities that lift your mood or that you enjoy – like taking a first sip of tea in the morning, being organized to get to work on time, a child's smile or cuddle, seeing a beautiful blossom, remembering your umbrella on a rainy day . . . everyone experiences fluctuations in mood in the course of any day. The recommended task here is to begin to notice such moments, no matter how fleeting, that are nourishing and help to lighten your mood, to value them and actively try to include more of them in your day.

Re-accessing expertise and developing skills

Past success, skill and expertise get forgotten when we are stressed out. Directing so much effort into trying to solve the problem of stress in our heads, as we are prone to do when feeling low, can result in making the problem even worse. It is therefore important to remind ourselves that thinking does not solve all problems and to actively decide to re-engage with doing either something that we enjoy or something that challenges us or gives us some sense of achievement once we accomplish it. It can be as simple a task as making a meal or completing a domestic chore, filling out a form, paying a bill that has been waiting for attention, doing the gardening or participating in a sporting activity, or even signing up for a new class or leisure activity that you have always wanted to do.

When 79-year-old Carole, whose beloved husband had died, began to remember the time when she was a dancer on stage, it was sufficient to engender in her a sense that, although 79, she could still join a local ballroom dance class and enjoy it.

Restoring a sense of personal competence or expertise, no matter how little, can redress the feeling of incompetence that is inherent to stress and help to improve your mood.

Initiate random difference

If it is simply too hard to engage in a pleasurable activity or to re-access any feeling of expertise, try this simple exercise that many people find helpful when low mood prevails. Most of us have routines in our lives which may be as simple as getting out of bed in the morning, showering and then having breakfast, in that order. Try to 'upset' the routine in some way. Have breakfast first and then shower. Other examples might entail finding another route to work, walking home along a different street, shopping at a different shop, sampling a new food, exploring a part of the countryside or city that is new to you.

To introduce difference at such a basic level can demand a creativity that is the antithesis of low mood, which is characterized by fixity of thought, feeling and behaviours. Introducing difference or surprise even at such an apparently insignificant level can bring the unexpected reward of feeling slightly more in control. If you allow yourself to experiment with 'newness' you will experience almost immediate positive feedback, such as the thought: 'If I can do this, perhaps there is more that I can do!' Any effort that contributes to introducing even a whisper of some returning sense of mastery or control is significant, valuable and helpful in alleviating some of the distress of low mood.

Rebuilding a sense of self-worth

The negative bias we have when our mood is low can filter out all our positive qualities, achievements, strengths, skills and resources. We become self-critical and discount and disqualify our own abilities, efforts, motivation, actions and capacity for endurance. Feelings of personal vulnerability, incompetence and failure can dominate our awareness. To begin to change this mindset is indeed a challenge. The following questions may help you with this process. We suggest that you have a notebook where you can write down and keep the answers:

- Name your three best qualities. (If this is impossible, write down the answers to the following questions first and then try this question again.)
- What difficulties have you had to overcome in your life?
- What did you do to overcome these difficulties?
- Who else knows what it took to overcome these difficulties?
- How did you learn to keep going?
- Did you learn to do this yourself or did someone else teach you?

It is helpful to begin to try to visualize yourself through the eyes of someone who really cares about you, either in the past or the present. If no such person exists it is helpful to imagine just such a person. The following questions can be used as a guide for this exercise, and we recommend that you write down your answers:

- What would that person who cares for you say about your best qualities, skills, efforts to overcome difficulties and challenges, your sense of humour, your ability to survive sticky situations?
- What are the qualities and skills you most appreciate in the person who cares for you?
- Which of these qualities do you see in yourself?

We suggest that you read through your answers to these questions on a daily basis. We suggest also that each day you add one or two things to the list that make you feel good. Note especially anything you have accomplished. Give yourself credit for the effort you invested and not just the results you achieved. Such events can be as apparently 'trivial' such as allowing someone else to speak ahead of you in a conversation, putting out the rubbish, allowing yourself the time to take a few minutes' break from the office, holding a door open so that someone can pass through ahead of you, telling yourself 'well done' for some task you managed to complete that you had been putting off. On Saturday morning we suggest you read through your diary for the week and see it as your present to yourself!

Noticing your negative thinking

When some or any of the above steps have been practised for some length of time, and hopefully with some shift for the better in terms of your mood, now may be the right moment to turn your thoughts to your thinking.

Try to begin to notice the connection between your thoughts and feelings

'I'm not thinking straight' is a phrase with which many of us are familiar. Our thoughts may be less than accurate when we are depressed or stressed out. It can be difficult for us to recognize this as we feel convinced of the accuracy of our thinking. After all, thinking serves us well in many aspects of our lives. It helps us to solve problems, to stay alive, to survive catastrophes, to dream dreams, to invent and create. Our thoughts and beliefs are our guide to living and interpreting life. They are the filter through which we experience life. Such a filter is made up of different and disparate aspects of our lives – childhood experience, personal circumstances, culture, innocent misunderstandings, traumatic happenings, myths, fancies, facts – a great amalgam of many different aspects of experience. No wonder, then, that at times our thinking can be faulty, extreme, disjointed and even add to our problems. The result may be that we can feel stressed, low or miserable.

The following case illustrates how thinking can make matters worse. A panic attack is part of the normal well-understood primal flight-or-fight process characterized by physiological arousal which prepares us to cope with challenge or danger. Sometimes our thinking can misconstrue this physiological arousal and this can add to our difficulties, as Mary's case illustrates.

Mary, an industrious and able student, first experienced chest pain when, without warning, the end of her university course deadline was brought closer. Mary began to think: 'I will be a failure,' 'I will no longer be a successful student,' 'I will never pass my exam now.' Such thinking compounded her physiological symptoms so that she began to experience more severe chest pain. Mary became increasingly aware of her heart beating and her chest constricting. She then began to think: 'I am having a heart attack.' She soon found herself in the emergency room of the local hospital requesting medical assessment. The above cycle repeated itself a few times in the ensuing weeks. Each time Mary sought medical help in the accident and emergency department she was given the reassurance that there was no medical problem with her heart. Eventually she was advised to see a counsellor. At this point the original problem with regard to course deadlines was almost lost from Mary's awareness. With the counsellor's help, Mary grew more aware of the role her thinking played in making her difficulties worse. When she began to think more calmly about her situation, she decided to see her tutor and negotiate an extension to her course deadline. She was able to then re-engage with her studies. Mary's chest pain began to lessen and eventually disappear. Figure 6.1 represents the process of Mary's anxiety.

Figure 6.1 Mary's anxiety

Problem: Course completion deadline brought forward.

↓

Mary experiences panic symptoms and chest pain, accompanied by the following thoughts: 'I will fail my degree.'

↓

'Objective' problem of enforced early course deadlines 'forgotten' by Mary as she experiences an increase in frequency and intensity of panic symptoms and chest pain, accompanied by the thought: 'Am I having a heart attack?'

↓

New problem emerges: 'Is there something wrong with my heart?' Mary visits the accident and emergency department with chest pain.

↓

Mary gets reassured that she does not have a medical problem with her heart and is referred to a counsellor for treatment of her panic symptoms.

↓

During the course of counselling Mary begins to grow more aware of how her catastrophic thinking has impacted on her situation.

↓

Mary speaks to her university supervisor to renegotiate her course deadline.

↓

Panic symptoms reduce, chest pain lessens and disappears.

↓

Mary re-engages with her studies.

It can be very helpful to begin to notice the role thinking plays in the construction and maintenance of stress, low mood and panicky or anxious feelings. When Mary began to 'notice' and challenge how her thinking impacted on her physical symptoms she began to understand her own role in making her problems worse. Cognitive behaviour therapy is a methodology that helps people to recognize, acknowledge and challenge what may be unhelpful beliefs or distortions in thinking, and helps create more positive and moderate beliefs that can contribute to improved mental health and well-being. There's an abundance of self-help material on this (see Useful addresses for details).

Becoming more aware of how unhelpful thinking affects our experience of life can be worthwhile. Such awareness is the first step in holding back from getting too caught up in thinking to the exclusion of other activities. It may be useful now to recall the funnel shape that represents this process, as mentioned at the beginning of this chapter. The benefits of daily relaxation and meditation practices are well understood to contribute to an increased capacity to be aware of our unhelpful thought processes without getting drawn into them.

If we begin to experience a drop in mood, the following checklist may be useful to have at hand so that we can begin to take action immediately:

- Am I getting enough sleep?
- Am I having a balanced diet?
- What exercise am I doing?
- What am I doing that I enjoy?
- Am I leaving enough time for my relationships and social life?
- Am I learning anything new?
- From what am I getting a sense of achievement?
- Do I have a structure to my day that includes relaxation or leisure time?
- Am I spending too much time caught up in my thoughts?

The objective of this chapter was to describe some proven and practical suggestions about what actions you can take yourself to improve, enhance or begin to restore your mental health and well-being on your own. It suggests alternatives to the problem of feeling miserable other than simply enduring it and getting exhausted by it. Having read this chapter, if it feels too difficult to get started on any of the changes outlined, this may be an indication that talking to a skilled professional such as a GP or therapist may be advisable.

7

Preparing for a first session of therapy

You have arrived at the point when your first therapy session is arranged. To have got this far, you have already thought a lot about your current situation and have probably made many efforts to solve your problem by yourself. Such efforts are not wasted and your courage and determination to change things has made you decide to seek professional help. You have already taken the important first step of realizing that there is a problem. Well done!

This chapter will help you to recognize and acknowledge the efforts you have made yourself to address your problem. It will help to guide you to best utilize the experience of therapy. It also attempts to summarize the most important things you need to think about and do before and after a first therapy session.

Research tells us that the more you put into the therapy the greater the return from it. Therapists do not have magical powers. Your input is essential. The more you can be clear, concise and explicit about your situation, the more likely it is that the therapist will be in a position to help you. This does not mean that you need to understand everything about your situation. Careful preparation, starting with addressing anxieties head on, will help you feel more grounded as your vulnerability or distress is going to be the focus of attention.

Prepare

Common anxieties

Questions and worries such as the ones listed below are common for people to ponder prior to taking the decision to see a therapist.

- Is my problem important enough? Other people's issues are graver than mine! I shouldn't be so self-indulgent.
- It's a failure on my part not to be able to solve my problem. If I try harder perhaps I could solve it myself.
- It's my own fault I feel so bad.
- Am I smart enough to talk to a therapist?
- Will I be exposing myself? I cannot ask for advice – she may think I'm stupid.
- What if I feel embarrassed or shy?
- Will I have to talk about my past?
- Will I have to lie on a couch?

Practically every person who meets with a therapist experiences some of these anxieties, or similar ones and it is part of the therapist's job to help you overcome them by making you feel at ease in talking about your problem. Knowing this, however, may not be sufficient to allay all your anxiety at this stage. Remember that feeling upset and stressed out is not the same as not coping. It is normal to feel anxious, upset or distressed in difficult or sad situations.

Thinking carefully beforehand about what it is that is bothering you and what it is you want to change in your life can lead to a more efficient use of time in a first therapy session.

The following questions may help you to focus on beginning to work through the issues that you wish to deal with. They can also help you to clarify your own feelings about the issues or problems you want to change.

- What do you feel is the issue or problem?
- How long has the issue been present in your life?
- Why do you think it is causing stress at this time in your life?
- What impact is it having on you; on people in your immediate and wider family; on your friends and colleagues?
- What do you think has made this issue persist?
- What has most helped to alleviate aspects of the problem? And what least?
- Are there any links between the problem that you are describing and previous difficulties or problems that you have encountered in your life?

- What words can you use to best describe it?
- What do you think could happen if it gets worse?
- What might you advise a friend who was experiencing a similar difficulty?
- What do you want to be different in your life?

Writing down the answers to these questions can help to sort out the muddle or confusion that often arises for us when things are difficult to deal with. Do not worry if you are unable to be clear about all problems or which problem is upsetting you most. Write a list of what you think are the main issues, how they are affecting you or others and your feelings about such issues. Bring them with you to the first meeting. The therapist will help you make sense of such issues.

Our mental health is closely connected with our physical health. Your ability to participate and gain from therapy will be greatly enhanced if you have begun to implement or restore some of the practical steps outlined in Chapter 6 of this book that are guaranteed to have a beneficial effect on both your physical and mental health, no matter how low you are currently feeling.

Practical arrangements

Sorting out as many practical issues as possible before your first therapy session will help reduce your anxiety and allow you to focus on the priorities when you sit face to face with a therapist. Below is a list of prompts to help your planning.

Have you confirmed the address of the therapist and the time of the meeting?

Do you know how to get there? Have you worked out how long it will take to get there? Arriving late and flustered for your first therapy session will increase your anxiety. Having too much waiting time may also increase your anxiety. Working out travel arrangements to and from the location of your therapist can be tricky in certain urban settings, so it is advisable to give it some thought beforehand. If you park your car on a parking meter, do leave sufficient time for the duration of your meeting. It is common for counselling sessions to last for 50 minutes, although this can vary depending on the therapist and context. Couple or family counselling sessions may last for more than an hour.

Have you thought about how you will fit time spent in counselling into your schedule?

Some therapists offer early morning or evening sessions. If you are seeing a therapist in a health care setting there may be less flexibility in terms of meeting times. Organization and forethought such as getting work or domestic chores completed on time may be necessary. Arrangements for your absence from work or home may require some thought or discussion with colleagues or family members.

Who needs to know about the fact that you are seeing a therapist?

Your employer? Partner? Colleague? Perhaps the wisest thing to do is to say little, and to as few people as possible, before you actually meet with your therapist. Your therapist should help you to find helpful ways to discuss with others the fact that you are seeing a therapist. Using 'talking therapies' as a means to overcome challenges and change your life for the better is becoming more and more acceptable.

How much will it cost?

Do you know if your counselling is free of charge, as in a health care context or an educational setting, or if you have to pay? Have you asked about the fee per session? Costs can vary greatly as there is no standard charge. It is important to know how much you will be paying before engaging in any contract with a therapist. Remember when working out your costs that the frequency of sessions comes into the tally. Some therapists work within a time-limited framework while others work with more open-ended contracts. Your therapist should supply you with this information prior to a first meeting.

What happens if you have to cancel an appointment?

Should you need to cancel a meeting, do you know whom to contact? How do you go about arranging a further meeting? Many settings now send text reminders to patients about appointment times. Cancellation may be done by text but you may need to telephone to make another appointment. If you are seeing a therapist privately you will need to ask the therapist directly about cancellation arrangements.

Is therapy confidential?

Everything you discuss with a therapist should remain between you and the therapist. Certain legal exceptions to this rule exist. The therapist should explain the detail of this in a first session. If you are seeing a therapist in a health care setting, such as a general practice, the therapist should explain to you what, if anything, will be noted on your medical record. Confidentiality is only breached at times where there is the gravest concern about your health and safety or that of others. All therapists need to have an external supervisor; this is a form of professional support to ensure their practice is safe, ethical and effective. Supervisors are bound by the same code of confidentiality.

If you do not already know the answer to any of these questions it may be a good idea to make a list and take them with you to your first meeting. Dealing with such practical issues in a matter-of-fact way with your therapist at a first meeting can help to ground you before you engage with what may be more painful issues. The way in which your therapist responds to these enquiries will also help you to get to know something about her and how she works.

Engage

During the therapy meeting

- Do not go to a counselling session feeling hungry! Therapy takes energy. Low blood sugar increases anxiety. Have a light snack before you go. Bring some water with you to drink if you know you are going to feel anxious.

- Do not be afraid to take the initiative. If something comes to mind that feels important, bring it to the therapist's attention. If it is important to you, it is important.
- Remember that different therapists have different styles. Some talk more than others. This is in part due to the fact that there are big differences between therapy approaches: in some, you will do most of the talking, while in others there will be much more of a dialogue. Still others, such as cognitive behavioural therapy, will involve you doing regular homework: some of this may be written, and sometimes it will require you to engage in some sort of planned behavioural change. If you have not already found out something about how your therapist approaches therapy it may be worth trying to do so now, or it could be on your list of questions for your first meeting.

After the therapy meeting

Therapy can be emotionally demanding and challenging. Nonetheless, it should not be so gruelling that it leaves you feeling even more stressed than you felt before you started the session. After a first therapy session, you may feel lots of different things. These should be broadly positive, even if all of the issues have not been fully addressed and the problem has not gone away. A first single session may not be enough time for longstanding, complex or sensitive problems to be overcome. It is helpful, however, to have some hope and optimism that your problem can be addressed with your therapist, and if this is not the case you may need to consider whether this is the right person or approach for you. Having confidence and a sense of trust in your therapist is an essential ingredient for a successful outcome.

Surveys of clients who have attended therapy suggest that you should feel or have experienced at least some of the following after a first session:

- a sense of being listened to and an awareness that you have not been 'directed' to think or feel differently;
- a sense of your therapist's professionalism: that she has given you her full and undivided attention throughout the session;

- a feeling of being 'connected' with the therapist: a sense of emotional warmth and closeness with her;
- some hope or optimism that you can either learn to live better with the problem or change it through therapy;
- some understanding of your problem or feelings and their impact on important parts of your life and relationships;
- an idea about how the therapist can help you, together with the likely time frame and outcome of therapy;
- a sense of how future sessions might work;
- guidance about 'homework' or any exercises that you may be able to do outside of sessions.

Sometimes you may get the feeling that things have not moved forwards in the way you would have liked in a first session. There may be many reasons for this. Sometimes it may be related to the skill of the therapist. Sometimes it may simply be too early to make this judgement. Sometimes you yourself may have had a part to play in a less than satisfactory outcome. If, for example, you have been hesitant or reticent and have not shared all of your feelings or difficulties with the therapist, this can make it difficult for her to help you. This is not a matter for self-criticism or harsh judgement – you may simply have felt too shy or overwhelmed at the time. However, it is important for you to recognize and acknowledge the nature of your own participation. Having thought about it, you can then decide what the possibilities are about being different when you meet the therapist again. Was there something really important that you failed to mention?

It is usually advisable not to 'over-think' a session of therapy too soon after the meeting ends. Often when we have unburdened ourselves about deep and painful issues we can feel somewhat vulnerable and low. It may be wise to treat yourself with some gentleness if this is so. Doing something relaxing (or nothing at all) immediately afterwards can help. If you have to return to work or domestic chores soon after your first therapy session, try to take at least 10 or 15 minutes to settle yourself before doing so. In the days after the meeting there will be time enough to reflect with more accuracy on the experience.

Commit

If your experience of a first session of therapy is positive then what is required of you now is taking the decision to continue and to commit to it. This will mean attending further sessions of therapy, coming well prepared, taking some responsibility for keeping therapy focused and productive, and completing any homework tasks that have been given. In the course of future meetings it is important to be honest if things arise that muddle or confuse you and to be unafraid to address them with your therapist. Ask for explanations when necessary. Giving feedback to your therapist about what works well for you is a sure way to keep your therapy 'on track'. It is very important that you trust your instinct and common sense. Remember, you are the customer.

How will I know if therapy is helping?

Trust your instinct and your feelings; feedback from friends or family can also help. If things are changing and improving, then therapy is working.

How long does therapy last?

Different approaches to therapy require different amounts of time to be effective. You will need to discuss with your therapist the length of time it might take for you to benefit from therapy and work out when you should review progress. This can range from a single session of therapy to several sessions per week over several years!

What happens after therapy ends?

What happens after therapy ends depends largely on the nature of the problem. It also depends on what else needs to be achieved, the progress you have made so far and life events at the time therapy ends. You may end therapy 'for good' or keep an open arrangement with your therapist to return if you need to. This may be for more work on the same problem or to address another one.

Conclusion

This book, so far, invites you to take a snapshot of your psychological or emotional state of health. We have offered many ideas and suggestions to help you do this. We have identified common psychological problems and given you some ideas based on up-to-date research about what you can do to help yourself. The Useful addresses section supplies more pointers towards accessing further self-help. This chapter has focused on how to prepare for a first therapy session, how to get the most out of it and guidance about how much therapy may be enough. No book, however, is a substitute for the experience itself.

Chapter 10 will focus on relaxation, exercise, sleep and nutrition, as we know that anxiety, feeling low and poor physical health can make any problem seem worse – if we are calmer, more relaxed and look after our physical needs we are more likely to make better and more informed decisions about whatever challenges we have to confront. First, however, we will take a look at online therapy and how and when it may be helpful.

8

Online therapy

A recent development in therapy has been through the use of the computer, where therapist and client may never meet face to face. For some people this is a real boon and for others it may not be appropriate. Let's start by looking at why people might find it helpful to access therapy this way.

Why choose to work online?

So why do some people choose to work online?

- Some choose it because of their geographic circumstances – they may live very far from any therapists.
- Public transport may be a problem.
- It may be difficult to leave home because of responsibility for care of the young or elderly.
- It is possible to access a therapist with a specialism not available in your locality – e.g. transgender issues or genetic counselling.
- For those who work shifts, particularly when these have a variable pattern, face-to-face therapy may be impractical.
- For those with a disability, mobility issues may lead to difficulties in accessing face-to-face premises or with using public transport; those with hearing difficulties may have no access to a signer, or because of the nature of the issue may not wish to have a third person (the signer) present in the room.
- Those who regularly travel for work may not be able to commit to ongoing face-to-face sessions. Using computers, they can continue work and still engage in counselling.
- In a few cases, clients may find it easier to talk about issues when they cannot see their therapist. It enables them to talk about feelings they regard as shameful.

- It may be easier to prevent family members knowing about therapy if you are not going out regularly to appointments.

Some myths about using computers for therapy

Because working this way is new, many people believe that it is second best. In our experience it is not better or worse, simply different. We need to remember that, going back into history, even Freud worked with some patients by means of letters. Using a computer is really only a similar process but without having to go to the post!

Another myth is that only people who cannot make relationships choose to work in this medium. If this was true it would suggest that online work would not help the client but rather reinforce the problem. However, we have found that it is indeed a myth. Our client range online is as great as the range we might meet face to face.

Some people say that the only reason for engaging in e-therapy is when it is impossible to access face-to-face counselling. This is perhaps an outdated concept. Increasingly, clients decide to engage in online therapy as a first choice. Use of the internet has become more and more a part of daily life; we regularly email and chat online to friends and family, we buy and bank online. The World Wide Web is used to access all kinds of information, and both computers and the internet are an integral part of the workplace. So using the internet for therapy does not seem to be such a difficult step. However, it may be wise to remember that not everyone is enthusiastic about using the internet. A lack of technological training and the fact that the older you are the less likely you are to be comfortable with computers are among reasons why some people may not use it. So you need to think carefully before you take this step or recommend it to a friend.

How does therapy work using the computer?

First, you need to know where to find an online therapist. The obvious place is on the internet! It may feel like taking a lucky dip, as you don't know how to judge whether the therapist is the right person for you. Later in the chapter, we'll look at how you can do this in the safest possible way.

There are a number of possibilities for using your computer for therapy. You could:

- work using emails;
- have live text sessions using Messenger or Skype;
- use the computer for voice conversations (just like using the telephone but through a service like Skype);
- use webcams for live sessions, so you and your therapist can actually see each other as well as reading what the other has written or hearing his or her voice.

Let's look at these in turn.

Email therapy

Your initial enquiry to a therapist about online counselling generally arrives in her email inbox. It may be of any length, and depending on your own style has varying amounts of detail. Some people just want to ask about how therapy will happen, while others will want the therapist to know quite a lot about their issue so they can make sure the therapist is competent to work with it.

Below are two examples of emails we have received:

1 I have visited your website and like what I saw. I am having a relationship problem. Would you be able to help me?

2 I am struggling to cope at work at the present. The future feels very uncertain, I might lose my job due to restructuring: and I am scared about what comes next. There is talk about the possibility of redundancy and this feels very bleak. I am not yet 50 and have ten years left on my mortgage. If the department are able to offer me another job it could be in any work area. I haven't done mainstream work for over ten years and the thought of retraining at my age is daunting.

I have noticed that I can be easily irritated at work, and when I go home I don't want to do anything. My partner has taken early retirement and he is enjoying this lovely weather. It is so hard to come in every day and just carry on.

Any help you can offer would be appreciated. I'm not sure how this will work . . . but I am willing to try anything that may make me feel a bit better. Can you tell me a bit more about how we would work together and what it would cost me please?

Thank you for listening.

Brenda

Although neither of these messages is long or has much detail, the second does give the therapist more to go on when replying. It also very sensibly asks about cost and how therapy would actually happen. It's important to ask questions just as you would face to face. In fact, a good online therapist won't start therapeutic work until you have sorted out practical details and are happy to agree a contract between you. The therapist will also probably ask quite a lot of questions about you before starting. These may seem intrusive or unnecessary, but remember that these are things that she would ask you during the first conversation face to face.

After these initial emails have been exchanged, you will get down to the therapeutic work. You and your therapist send emails back and forth, usually at agreed times of the week. You may have agreed a certain number of email exchanges or work with an open contract. In that respect, it's the same as face-to-face work.

Therapists will reply in various ways. Some may send a new email back that picks up points you have made and explores them further with you. Others will use email dialogues with you, where they write back to you within the email you sent, making additions in a different font or a different colour so these are clear. Here is part of an email reply.

Client: I don't know where to begin today. I'm worried about my marriage, my children, my mother. I just seem to have stopped thinking again . . . I just hope you can help me sort myself out. It's all such a muddle.

Therapist: Do you think it might help if you try and focus on just one thing? . . . I really want to say 'slow down, take a deep breath; let's talk through things one at a time.' But that may not be how you see it, so let me know what's right for you. I'm going to ask an odd question – when you stop thinking, what are you doing instead?

Using live sessions online

To set up this way of working, you need both access to the internet and a chat room that is private and secure. Some therapists set up their own chat or conference rooms on their websites or join a service such as Messenger or Skype. These are free downloadable software packages, enabling you to 'talk' to your therapist at a pre-arranged time in a private space. It can only be accessed by one participant inviting another into the 'room'. No-one else can intrude on your conversation by mistake. Many readers will already use Messenger and Skype to keep in touch with friends and family, so will feel familiar with working this way.

Using live chat doesn't mean that you and your therapist can talk whenever you feel like it simply because you see she is online! Part of your contracting will have been around times of appointments. In practice, some therapists do have an agreement that if they are online and the client is in crisis contact is possible, but this is unusual and solely applies to crisis.

A session usually lasts around an hour, just like face-to-face sessions. One drawback of working this way might be if you or your therapist are very slow typists. Then you may feel impatient about how little you are able to 'talk' during a session. On the other hand, sometimes this can give you time to reflect on what you and your therapist are writing to each other.

Here is a typical extract from a session.

Client: *We have now made the decision not to move, which I am pleased about. And I want to sort out my career plans too.*

Therapist: Marty, just before looking at your career plans, could I just check out something about your decision?

Client: *Sure.*

Therapist: I'm not sure whether you meant that you were pleased that you'd decided against moving, or whether you meant that you were pleased to have got a decision made. I know being in limbo around the decision has been difficult for you, so wanted to check which you meant. Hope that's OK to ask?

Using the computer like a telephone

Therapy in this way is exactly like phone therapy, except that you use an internet service such as Skype instead of a landline or mobile phone. Your computer needs to have either a built-in microphone and speaker, or external ones attached. This is easily done using a headset. Obviously you need to download the program from the internet, but this is simple to do. The main advantage of using this form of 'telephone' therapy is that calls are free (if you are in the UK) or very cheap (if you are calling to or from outside the UK). Many people find it less physically intrusive as you don't need to hold a phone to your ear for an hour. Another advantage could be that it won't show up on phone bills, which could be important if you don't want others to know about your therapy. For some people, it is a good compromise between face-to-face and online work. They can hear their therapist and know that their voice is being heard, even if they cannot be seen.

Using webcams

Using a webcam allows you to see your therapist and be seen by her. Some computers have built-in cameras, but more often you attach an external one and position it so you can send your image in real time to the therapist. You can use a webcam with Skype in addition to voice conversations, and you can use it during a live chat (text) session. There are advantages and disadvantages to using webcams. The greatest advantage for many people is that they feel more connected to the other person if they can see him or her. Of course, occasionally that may be exactly what someone is trying to avoid when seeking therapy using the internet. The disadvantages are mainly due to technology. How good the images are will depend on the quality of the equipment and the speed of the internet. If your broadband speed is slow or you use a dial-up connection, then images can be very jerky and off-putting. Also, if either of you looks at the keyboard when you type, then the other person may not be able to see you very well. Technology is improving all the time and using webcams will probably increase over the next few years.

Using text messaging

Very occasionally, therapy will be offered solely by text message from a mobile phone. This is unusual because of the limited amount that can be written at any one time, and sometimes because of the cost. However, increasingly therapists and clients use text for emergency contact, so it can be worth discussing this with your therapist.

So what are the problems with online therapy?

Like almost everything, there are important issues to consider before choosing this way of working. The first is to do with *qualifications*. In our opinion, it is not enough for someone simply to be a qualified therapist in order to work online. People also need extra training to be able to work in this different way. You wouldn't want a general practitioner to carry out major surgery on you, so apply the same common sense here. You can ask about this or you may be able to check by visiting the therapist's website.

A useful way of finding an online therapist is to visit the website of the Association of Counsellors and Therapists Online (www.acto-uk.org). All therapists listed there must have had additional training in online work, and also conform to a special code of ethics for working with online clients.

Obviously, working online makes it easy to work across national boundaries. In some ways this is great, as you can access a therapist speaking your native language, or with the same cultural background. The one thing to consider is what you would do if you needed to take some action or make a complaint.

The professional organizations might not be the same, and you would almost certainly be taking action under a different legal system. This probably sounds a little over the top, as very few therapists and clients get into these types of problems, but is perhaps something just to consider.

The other crucial area is *security*. There are two main aspects to this. The first concerns privacy when working with your online therapist. It is very easy to overlook the basics here. You'll need a private space to write your emails or take part in a live session. It would be unhelpful to have friends or family looking over your shoulder as you type, or even simply coming in and out of the room and disturbing you. On the other hand, will the family think it odd if you shut yourself away with the computer if they don't know that you are engaging in therapy?

Never be tempted to use a computer in your workplace for therapeutic purposes, as it is possible for employers to access emails. Occasionally clients have successfully used internet cafés or a public library for therapeutic work – if you use a secure encrypted system this can be theoretically safe, but there is still the problem of being in a public place.

The other aspect is the security of your computer. If you are going to engage in therapy, you do want to make sure that no-one else can access what you have written either in emails or in the history of a live chat session. If you don't do this, you may find that you censor what you write in case anyone else reads it, and that won't be helpful. So the first thing is to 'password protect' your computer (or, on a shared computer, your personal area of it). Avoid choosing a password that all the family will know!

Many therapists recommend that you set up a special email address specifically for your therapeutic work. This ensures that you access it when you wish to and that your therapeutic work doesn't come into your main inbox, where you might be tempted to open it even though you know you haven't really got time to read the reply. Some people (clients and therapists) choose to write their responses as a Word document and attach them to an email in order to avoid 'open' therapeutic emails.

It is easy to set up a system to encrypt your emails – that is to say, they cannot be read by anyone else as a password is needed to render them readable. A free system many therapists use is Hushmail, but there are others. These are web-based services, so you have to log on through the web and the emails will not come into your usual inbox. Skype is also a secure encrypted system. Remember to ask your therapist about his or her security arrangements, as you don't want your emails not being secure at that end either.

Web-based therapeutic programs

There are therapeutic programmes on the web, available for anyone to use, and some popular ones are listed in the Useful addresses.

Conclusion

Online therapy or e-therapy is an expanding area of therapy. There are advantages and disadvantages, as you will have realized. We have talked about it here as if it is a separate entity from face-to-face therapy, but of course it is possible to use both ways of working, sometimes working online and sometimes face to face. Talk to your therapist about how you would like to work, and ask all the questions you need answered before you start. Then, if it seems a good option for you, go for it, with your eyes wide open to things you need to consider to make it work well for you.

9

For friends and family

When friends or families see someone they love in distress, there is usually a huge desire to comfort and help them. Sometimes that is easy to do, as when there is a practical solution to a problem. For example, if the problem is accommodation, we may be able to put someone up for a short time, or lend money for the rent for a week. We might know someone who could help – a builder for repairs, or a social worker for advice. Or last, we may know where to signpost the person – the Citizens Advice Bureau or an advocacy service, for example.

It is much more difficult when the issue has a high emotional content and this is the main cause of distress. Then we can feel more helpless and out of our depth. And if you are a parent worried about a child, there may also be a feeling of guilt. 'I ought to be able to help. This is my child, after all, and if I can't help, who can?' In fact, sometimes parents are the least likely to be able to help as they are so closely involved. Also, remember that, despite our good intentions, we may be part of the problem!

Step 1: Finding out if there *is* a problem

There is a tendency among friends and family to rush into 'doing' things, or organizing people. So the first thing we suggest is that you slow down for a minute. Ask yourself the extremely difficult question: 'Do I want him to get help because *he* wants it? Or is it that I will feel better and less anxious if I know he has a professional helping him?'

Of course, it is usually a mixture of both. However, if there is any of the latter present, it is a good time to take a deep breath, stand back a little, and see if you can do some listening. There is a wonderful card that says 'What you really need is a good listening to!' Yes, a '*listening* to' rather than a '*talking* to' or, even worse, a 'talking *at*'. If we can just listen to our friend or relative, we may be able to discover what help he needs from professionals – if any. We may discover that he has greater tolerance for withstanding this emotional distress than we have, and actually is coping well enough. Alternatively, he may be immobilized and unable to take action. Yet again, he may not share our concern. What we are really saying here is 'Whose problem is it – his or yours?'

Without wanting to sound patronizing, we need to stress that it is actually very difficult to listen well. Good listening means that we have to concentrate on the other person and keep our own thoughts to ourselves. Some of the major barriers are:

- switching off if we think we've heard it before or have the answer;
- judging what is being said against what *we* might do or feel;
- interrupting before understanding;
- picking up details rather than main themes;
- faking interest;
- being distracted;
- reacting emotionally.

What we need to do instead is to encourage the person to speak by conveying warmth and interest. It helps to accept the other person's feelings and not to judge or try to change them. We can show we've heard by reflecting back what we think has been said to us, and checking out whether we've got it right or not.

Once you start saying, 'Yes, but . . .' you are trying to get the person to see things your way and not his own, before you've actually shown that you do understand what is being said. It's unhelpful if you ignore emotions, but it can be equally unhelpful to enter into the emotion so much that you smother the person and don't enable him to shout or cry or do whatever he needs to do.

You may think you have the answer or solution to the problem, but suggesting this too soon is going to be counter-productive. It turns people off, as they feel you want them to adopt your solution regardless of whether it's right for them or not. The same thing happens if you diagnose ('Oh, I can see why you think that – you've never had a good relationship with your mother') or generalize ('Most people feel like that'). You may be spot on, but before your thoughts are accepted people need to know that you have heard them fully.

If you watch political debates on television you will see many examples of bad listening – in fact, not listening at all! The speakers and interviewers are not interested in what the other is saying, but want to get their own point across. As a result, people get angry or frustrated, or tune out.

Step 2: Knowing whether professional help is needed

Once you've listened to someone, you are in a much better position to know how best to help. You may find that offering space to talk without being offered solutions or advice has actually been enough, and that he says something like, 'That was really helpful. I feel so much better, as if a great weight has been lifted off my shoulders.'

Occasionally people may say how much they value what you have said, even though you may not really have said anything much! This is because in the space where you have been listening, they have 'heard' themselves, and worked out how they want to go forward. Sadly, we don't often give time to listening to ourselves.

However, assuming that more is needed, you have to consider whether you'd like to help the person find professional help, or whether that is not appropriate at this stage. For example, let's imagine that your friend has been bereaved. It is perfectly natural to feel lost, angry, numb, depressed, overwhelmed, etc., if you have been recently bereaved. So what your friend may need is a space to talk without feeling that he 'shouldn't be going on', and perhaps for you to reassure him that what he is feeling is natural – after all, if he was close to the person who died, it would be very odd if he wasn't feeling all these things.

The bereavement charity Cruse often suggests that unless the circumstances are unusual, people wait for at least three to six months before deciding whether they need counselling or not. By 'unusual', we mean such things as traumatic death, or perhaps the sudden death of a child, or a death that re-awakens memories of old losses, in a way that feels too difficult to contain.

Some of the things that might alert you to someone needing professional support are:

- the person being unable to switch off from anxiety;
- the person not being able to carry out usual tasks or work;
- irritability;
- being more aggressive or more passive than usual;
- eating and sleeping patterns being disturbed for more than a few days;
- increased use of alcohol, over-the-counter medication or other substances;
- ignoring personal hygiene;
- withdrawing from social contact;
- changes in behaviour;
- headaches, nausea and unexplained aches and pains.

Just because a person displays one of these signs, however, does not mean he necessarily needs help. It is more likely if there is a cluster of indications.

It is particularly difficult for parents to decide if their children need professional support. Often children find it hard to confide in their parents, and parents can be so concerned about their children that they can find it impossible to simply listen and then make a decision. There are all sorts of questions that also arise about whether to accept what the child says, like, 'I don't want you to do anything about the bullying as that will make it worse. And if someone even sees me going to talk to the counsellor, they'll call me a loser.' Do you go along with this or override it?

US authors Adele Faber and Elaine Mazlish have written two books that are particularly useful for parents struggling to communicate with children and young people: *How to Talk So Kids Will Listen and Listen So Kids Will Talk* and *How to Talk So Teens Will Listen and Listen So Teens Will Talk* (for details, see Further reading).

Though some of the language may seem a little over the top for a UK readership, the content is very sound. In fact, much of what is said applies to talking to anyone, not just children! The ideas in these books are also useful when we simply find ourselves in difficulties communicating with the young, not just when there are major problems.

Step 3: Encouraging others to seek professional help

So having listened well and decided that your friend or relative would benefit from professional help, the next step is to find that help. But wait one more minute – in fact the next step is to discover whether the person involved agrees with you. You may well be right; professional help would be valuable. However, if he doesn't feel it is necessary, either he is not going to make a move to seek it or if he does he will do so reluctantly, possibly sabotage it, and then blame you for it being of no help at all!

So you need to find ways of encouraging the person to seek help without him feeling he is being frog-marched into something for your benefit. Some ways you might try are:

- simply asking him if he has thought of any ways forward, or of professional help he might seek – and listening genuinely to the answer;
- if he is open to this, you could suggest that you sit together and make a list of all possible sources of support or help;
- you could ask him about the pros and cons of the sources that he or you both have thought of;
- ask him how he'd begin to find out more about the resources he has listed, within his locality;
- encourage him to see his GP, where he may be able to access free counselling.

It is easy to fall into the trap of rushing into contacting professionals without having really understood what help the individual is seeking and without involving him in the decision. We usually do this from the best and most kind-hearted motives, but it would be much better for us to stand back and support someone's efforts rather than do it for him. Of course, occasionally, we may be asked to do something because there are difficulties in our friend making the first move. Then we gladly do it, but it's important to check exactly what we are being asked to do, so that we do it as the person wishes, and not in our 'better' way!

Step 4: The different types of help available

There are a number of different options available, and not all of them will be right for everyone. There is a list of resources at the back of this book you might want to look through (see Useful addresses). Also, think about what you know about your friend or relative and the ways in which that person prefers to operate – some people prefer to work on their own with a self-help book or a computer package, others will prefer to talk to someone, while yet others would rather work in a group.

Although the chapter on choosing a therapist was written for the person seeking therapy, you may find it useful to read it yourself, so you have some idea of the process as well. This helps you support your friend in the process of deciding what to do and who to choose. Therapy can happen in a number of ways. The main ones are listed below.

Self-help groups

These are usually arranged for a number of people who all want to overcome or deal with a particular problem or issue – alcohol or drug dependency, depression, anxiety, bereavement or eating disorders, for example. Quite often, though not always, these groups are led by people who have overcome the same difficulty themselves. These groups are not for everyone, as your relative or friend will be expected to share personal experiences in the group, and to learn from and encourage other participants. If the person you are supporting hates social situations, this won't be his preferred option. These groups are sometimes free; if there is a charge this is usually lower than individual counselling as costs are shared between participants.

Individual counselling

As its name suggests, this takes place in a series of meetings between a counsellor and a client, in a private space. Meetings usually last about 50–60 minutes. Some therapists specialize in a particular area, such as abuse, work-related issues or relationships, while others offer a broad approach to issues they can work with. The counsellor will not give advice or tell your friend what to do, but will help him find his own best way forward.

Some free counselling is available through the NHS or voluntary agencies, though there may be a waiting list for these services. Independent counsellors do make a charge, and as the therapy might go on for a few months, you will need to think about whether your friend or family member can afford this before helping him to embark on this course.

Couple or relationship counselling

This is for couples wanting to look at their relationship. You need to know whether your friend thinks his partner might be prepared to go with him. Often, even when one person is willing to go, the other may not see the need – or even not agree there is a problem. Relate is possibly the best known agency for relationship work, but many independent counsellors also offer work with couples. Encourage your friend to go to someone with specific training in this area.

There is also *family therapy*, where the dynamics of the whole family are explored, with the aim of helping that family to live more effectively together. It is possibly the least easy form of therapy to access, so before thinking about helping your friend to go along this route, find out about possibilities within your local area, perhaps through your GP or the NHS Trust. That way you avoid firing up the individual and possibly family members, only to find the reality is that either it's not available at a reasonable cost or there's a year's waiting list.

Step 5: Making contact with a therapist

The hard work is done. You've helped your friend or family member to sort out what he wants to do. You and he have come up with options. Now all that has to happen is for him to make contact with the professional and set up an initial appointment. You may expect this to happen quickly, but there is often a pause at this point. It's almost as if once people have decided what to do, they need a period of standing back and just allowing themselves time before going any further. This can be frustrating for you, having worked with him so well to encourage him to reach this point. As you will have guessed by now, our advice is to let him take the time he needs. Yes, ask if he wants any help in making this first contact, but try not to pressurize. Of course, this isn't true of everyone, and some people are perfectly happy to go forward immediately.

As a general rule, therapists prefer the person who will be the client to make the contact to set up the appointment. This is because they want to make sure that the individual really does want to come into therapy, and isn't being forced into it in any way.

However, if it is desired by the client and would be helpful, there is nothing to prevent you doing some of the donkey-work beforehand. You could check availability and fee structures of a number of practitioners, as well as whether they work with the particular issue. Then the client makes the next step of contacting someone for an appointment.

An exception to that general rule would be if a young person is involved. It seems reasonable that parents might want to check a professional before making an appointment on behalf of their child. There are some youth counselling agencies where young people from about the age of 11 can self-refer, but many appointments with therapists in independent practice would involve the parent or guardian at this point. The therapist may want this as well as the parent.

Step 6: When therapy begins

Again, most practitioners prefer to see the client alone, without a friend or family member present. However, there is nothing to stop you going with the person to the location, if he feels nervous or anxious. You could then wait in the car or a local café with a book, until the appointment is finished.

The exception once more is a parent with a child. Then you might want to accompany the child in to see the therapist, particularly if the child is very young. You probably would only stay in the room for a few minutes, but most practitioners recognize that a parent may want to see them and possibly check out some practical details, like timing for picking the child up again, paying the counsellor, etc. Obviously, it will also depend on the child or young person. Your child may not wish you to come into the therapy room, and it would be wise to respect his or her autonomy. You may need to give the child a cheque, though, to be able to pay, and make sure you have agreed where you will meet up afterwards!

And finally . . . let him get on with it

The last hurdle is treading the fine line between being interested in the process and appearing to want to know what is happening. Perhaps the easiest way to deal with this is to be quite open. 'I am very happy that you tell me about your therapy if you want to, but I know it is for you, and I don't need to know anything at all. Maybe from time to time, I might just say "How's it going?" and you can say "Fine" or say more if you want! Is that OK?'

Because this is *not* your therapy, and if you have done a good enough job in supporting your friend to find the necessary help, that is sufficient and you can be pleased with how you've handled this. Remember, the skill is offering support if and when it is asked for, and not smothering someone or taking over.

Just because someone is experiencing psychological difficulties just at the moment doesn't mean that he should be treated like a child or is incompetent. Instead, help him to utilize his skills effectively to seek the type of help he needs. Seeking help is a sign of competence, not failure or weakness.

10

Help with relaxing, exercising, sleep and eating habits

In this chapter we highlight three of the most commonly arising psychological symptoms or problems that affect almost everyone at some time in their lives, namely:

1 stress, tension or anxiety;
2 sleep disturbance;
3 eating difficulties.

There are many self-help books and online services that can also assist you with this and some of these are listed at the back of the book. The emphasis in this chapter is on what you can do by yourself to start the process of using relaxation skills, physical exercise, sleep improvement techniques and reviewing your eating patterns, to enhance your overall ability to cope and improve your mood and mental well-being. If you have questions or concerns about any of the issues or suggestions made in this chapter, do first check them with your therapist, practice nurse or GP.

Learning how to relax

Learning relaxation skills can help you gain a sense of calm, control and confidence. They can also help you to cope with stressful and difficult situations. Learning how to control bodily symptoms of anxiety is a skill that needs be practised frequently before you can experience lasting benefits and mastery. It is a bit like learning to drive a car: you need to keep practising until you are able to co-ordinate the many skills required to operate the vehicle without consciously thinking about them. This section presents a number of relaxation techniques to help to reduce anxiety, stress and tension. We first focus on relaxed, controlled ways of breathing before moving on to how to release physical tension and relax your body and mind.

Relaxed, controlled breathing

We tend to over-breathe whenever we are tense or exercising. This is a mild form of hyperventilation that increases blood circulation so that our muscles can be primed to react during activity. Our heart rate increases, our breathing becomes more regular and muscles may tense up slightly. Rapid breathing is not problematic in the short term. It is a perfectly healthy response to ensure we can sustain exercise, whether working out in the gym, running a marathon or speeding towards the office to make the morning meeting. It is also a normal response to stress and anxiety.

The overall goal of the breathing technique below is to learn a way to relax through breathing. This involves practising taking gentle, even breaths that fill your lungs completely, and exhaling in a slow manner. Start by practising this technique in a comfortable situation when you are not too stressed or anxious. Each exercise should last for about ten minutes and ideally be practised twice a day if you can, once in the morning and once in the evening.

- Before starting, it is important that you feel comfortable. Practise controlled breathing in a seated position with your hands relaxed on either side of your body, or with your back flat on the ground in a lying position.
- Loosen any tight clothing and take off your shoes if you can.
- Let your shoulder blades sink down your back and lean slightly towards the back of the chair (or the ground if you are lying down) to support your back. Close your eyes.
- Start by taking a deep breath in through your nose and exhale slowly through your mouth. Continue to breathe in this way five more times.
- Try to make each inhalation and exhalation of the same duration. When you inhale, count slowly from 1 through to 4.

Do the same when you exhale so that you are breathing evenly in a slow and focused manner. Notice how your breathing is slowing down.

- Your heart beat should now be slowing down too. Your arms and legs are relaxed. Continue to count slowly from 1 to 4 on each inhalation and then again for each exhalation.
- Let go of all bodily tension. Continue to breathe deeply five more times . . . in through your nose and out through your mouth. Feel the quietness and peacefulness around you.
- Slowly open your eyes. Continue to breathe gently and evenly in through your nose and out through your mouth. If you are in a seated position, raise your arms upwards and stretch the whole of your body upwards. If you are lying down, flex your arms and legs downwards and gently move back up into a seated position.

You may find it a challenge to practise controlled breathing at first. It may feel as if you are not getting enough air or that the pace of your breathing seems unnaturally slow. This is a normal reaction when you practise a new routine. As your confidence and skill improve and you learn to relax more quickly, you will find it easier to switch to correct breathing whenever you feel stressed or anxious.

Releasing physical tension

Once you have learned the skill of relaxing your muscles, your mind and body will automatically feel calmer. It is almost impossible for the mind to be tense when the body is relaxed. The ability to relax is not always something which comes easily; it is a skill that needs to be learned gradually and practised regularly. The aim is to learn relaxation techniques in advance so that you are in a better position to manage stress or anxiety. Relaxation methods have a very good chance of success if you practise them regularly.

Monitoring progress

Before you begin to practise relaxation skills, spend a minute or two identifying the intensity of your stress and anxiety levels. This could be done by asking yourself: how tense or stressed or anxious do I feel right now? Copy Table 10.1 into your notebook, and use a scale from 1 (low) to 10 (high) to rate the degree of tension, stress or anxiety.

Table 10.1 Measuring your tension, stress and anxiety levels

How tense, stressed or anxious do I feel?	Before relaxation 1 (low) – 10 (high)	After relaxation 1 (low) – 10 (high)
Tense		
Stressed		
Anxious		

Work through the exercise below. Once you have finished the exercise, measure your anxiety again. Compare the scores and see whether you feel less (or no change) in your tension, anxiety or stress levels after completing the relaxation sequence. Repeat this procedure for each of the exercises provided. You need to know if the relaxation procedure works for you.

Progressive muscular relaxation

This exercise teaches you to make a distinction between tensed and relaxed muscles, which helps you to identify when you are tense so that you can learn to relax your muscles. Muscular tension can occur automatically as a reaction to uncomfortable thoughts and worry. We are not always conscious of physical tension and it is therefore not uncommon to experience prolonged periods of muscular strain. The sequence is quite simple and takes you through all parts of your body. This exercise is best done in a lying position, but if this is difficult sitting in a chair can work equally well. You can use the controlled breathing techniques in the previous exercise (see p. 85) to enhance relaxation and calmness.

The basic movements for each part of your body are as follows: tense the muscles as much as you can and concentrate on feeling the strain within your body. Hold the tension for about five seconds and then release your muscles. Relax for 15 seconds and note the difference between the tense and relaxed state of your muscles. Use this basic technique on each of the muscle group in turn. Remember to breathe gently and evenly throughout the exercise.

- *Hands* Clench your left hand and make a tight fist. Then relax your left hand – let it sink towards the ground. Do the same with your right hand.
- *Arms* Tense your whole arm. Imagine holding a set of weights in your hand. Bring the bottom half of your arm upwards as this makes it easier to flex your arm. Relax for 15 seconds. Repeat the process for your other arm.
- *Face* Tense your eyebrows by frowning, then your forehead, finally your jaw. Relax for 15 seconds and repeat.
- *Neck and shoulders* Let your chin drop down towards your chest. Squeeze your shoulders up towards your neck as hard as you can. Hold for 15 seconds and then relax. Repeat the process one more time. As your shoulders release, feel your shoulder blades slide gently down your back towards your waist.
- *Abdomen* Tighten the muscles in your stomach by pulling them in and up. Hold for five seconds and then relax for 15 seconds. Repeat the tensing and relax again.
- *Thighs* Relax your upper body. Tighten your thigh muscles by squeezing buttocks and thighs together. Relax for 15 seconds before repeating the process.
- *Legs* Bend your feet downwards so that your toes are pointing towards the floor. There should be a tightening sensation in the back of your leg muscles. Relax for 15 seconds. Then bend your feet the other way so that your toes are pointing upwards. You should feel a light tension in the front part of your legs. Relax.
- *The whole of your body* Tense all of the above body parts all at once. You should feel a tension in your hands, face area, neck and shoulders, abdomen, thighs and legs. Relax for 15 seconds and then repeat this process once more.

Take care to not over-tense muscles as this can cause discomfort or even injury to your body. Remember to breathe slowly and regularly between each part of the exercise. Before standing up straight, gently stretch and move your arms and legs, avoiding any sudden or jerky movements. When ready, take your time standing up. If you still feel tense at the end of the exercise try and go through the sequence once more. Remember, it takes time to learn how to relax.

The benefits of regular exercise

The value of physical exercise in the maintenance of health is difficult to overestimate. The Chief Medical Officer in the UK recently stated that if there were a drug available with all the beneficial effects of physical activity, it would be greatly sought after!

The positive effects of regular exercise:

- Exercise can have a positive effect on mood. Exercise stimulates various brain chemicals, which can leave you feeling happier and more relaxed than before working out.
- Exercise delivers blood, oxygen and nutrients to your tissues. In fact, regular exercise helps your entire cardiovascular system work more efficiently.
- Regular exercise can help you fall asleep faster and deepen your sleep.
- Exercise has a positive effect on your health, weight and overall vitality.

When you feel stressed out and your mood is low, you may find that any kind of activity becomes a challenge. It is important to set small, manageable goals for yourself, such as:

- getting out of the house each day, even for a brief period;
- going for a brisk walk;
- alighting one stop early from public transport and walking to your destination;
- walking up a set of stairs instead of taking the lift or escalator;
- going to the gym;
- going for a run;
- mountain walking;
- cycling;
- ballroom dancing;
- attending a yoga class.

Getting up from a sitting or lying position to change a TV channel instead of using a hand-held remote control could be a first step to re-establishing movement in your life.

It is important to select the type of exercise that appeals most or requires the least effort. It really does not matter what form it takes, but it is most beneficial when sufficiently vigorous so that your heart rate is increased for at least 20–40 minutes per session of exercise. A programme of three sessions per week, lasting about 45 minutes each, is an optimum recommended level to maintain health. It is good to aim for at least 30 minutes a day of any gentle activity. This may take a number of weeks to work up to, or even longer. The important thing is that you start doing something immediately, no matter how little this is. Do not be discouraged if this doesn't seem much at first. Sometimes it is helpful to schedule exercise in at the same time each day. The chances are that if an activity is not scheduled, negative thinking can begin to overwhelm you. It is better to move first and think later! We recommend that you exercise earlier rather than later in the day, as exercising late in the day may not help sound sleep. Persist and you will be rewarded with the benefits of exercising, physically and emotionally.

Helpful hints on how to improve sleep

Sleeping well helps us to enjoy life and cope better, and is necessary to maintain sound mental health and well-being. There is no golden rule, however, about how much sleep is required each day as it varies from person to person. Our requirement for sleep usually lessens with age. Sleep problems are a common feature of feeling low, stressed out or anxious. Indeed, disturbed sleep is often the symptom that prompts people to seek professional help.

People experience difficulties with:

- going to sleep;
- staying asleep;
- waking up too early;
- interrupted sleep;

- not feeling rested or refreshed by sleep;
- having thoughts such as 'I'm going to lie awake all night' or 'I worry that I will not be able to cope tomorrow if I don't get a good night's sleep.'

If you have a problem with sleep it is a good idea to start keeping a sleep diary. Each day for about a week, record:

- what you do in the two or three hours before bedtime;
- the time you go to bed;
- the time it takes to go to sleep;
- what you do if you wake up during the night;
- the time of waking up in the morning;
- the time of getting up in the morning;
- how rested you feel when you get up.

Sleep difficulties can have a number of causes:

- medical issues such as pain or bladder conditions;
- certain medications (steroid treatment can make some people wakeful for long periods, and other medications may cause vivid and upsetting dreams);
- change in sleep routine (shift work, prolonged or excessive working hours, jet lag, travel fatigue and unanticipated events such as illness can all affect the quality and duration of sleep);
- ageing;
- upsetting life events, e.g. bereavement;
- stress and mood problems (when we feel stressed, worried or anxious, sleep deprivation or too much sleep can follow);
- environmental factors, such as uncomfortable bedding, inadequate temperature control in the bedroom, noise levels either within the sleeping area or external to it.

The suggestions below are to help you to establish, maintain or restore a healthy waking and sleeping routine. When you complete your own sleep diary you will have a clearer picture of any particular issues and so may find some suggestions more relevant than others.

Environment

- Aim to associate your bedroom only with sleep and relaxation.
- Make your sleep environment as comfortable as possible to suit your own preferences, including bedding, temperature control and noise levels.
- Leave disputes and conflict with your sleep partner at the bedroom door!
- Banish these activities from your sleep area: watching TV, listening to lively music, eating, drinking, smoking.

Establish a pre-sleep routine

- Aim to go to bed at around the same time every night.
- Set the alarm for the same time each morning. As soon as the alarm goes off, get out of bed, whatever the quality or duration of your sleep. Do not stay in bed longer to 'catch up' on sleep. If you prolong lying in bed for erratic intervals, this jeopardizes the wake–sleep body rhythm you are trying to establish.
- Aim to do physical exercise earlier rather than later in the day.
- Avoid napping during the day.
- Avoid coffee or other caffeinated drinks close to your sleep time.
- Have a warm drink such as a herbal tea or a malty milk drink.
- Avoid 'heavy' meals or spicy food.
- Take a warm bath, play relaxing music, listen to a relaxation tape, practise physical relaxation just prior to going to bed.
- Keep the face of your clock covered. Checking the time can wake you up.

If you are unable to fall asleep or you wake up in the night, try not to worry. People worry much more than they need to about sleep loss. Do the relaxation exercises described earlier. Keep breathing slowly and evenly. Thinking about a relaxing or pleasant situation or experience can reduce tension. If after 30 minutes you are still unable to sleep, get up and leave the bedroom if possible. Engage with some non-stimulating activity such as making a warm drink, reading or listening to soothing music or a relaxation tape. Return to bed when you feel sleepy.

Medical problems

If you experience symptoms such as pain, breathlessness, upset stomach, needing to use the toilet frequently or other problems that interrupt your sleep, do discuss these with your doctor.

Change in sleep routine

If your life involves major sleep routine changes due to shift work or frequent long-haul travel, it is helpful to anticipate potential adverse effects. A useful practice might include delaying your return to work after a long-haul trip by a day or half a day, whenever possible.

Ageing

Do not accept disturbed or interrupted sleep as something to be endured in later life without first seeking medical advice. Find out if this really is a sleep problem or if another problem is causing you to lose sleep.

Getting ready for sleep

Preparation for the next night's sleep begins as soon as we get up in the morning. What we do, think and feel, and our attitude to life between one night's sleep and the next, affects how we sleep. We generally sleep less well when feeling low or anxious. We wake up tired so we do less. Because we feel tired we cut down on all kinds of activities, including physical exercise. We give up on social or leisure activities which normally can help us relax. We may even be tempted to nap during the day. The result is, we sleep less well. A vicious cycle gets established. Read again some of the self-help suggestions in Chapter 6 – beginning to do any of those can help to break the vicious cycle that has been set up and can contribute to sleeping more soundly.

Improve your eating: 'we are what we eat' and it's not 'all in the mind'!

These two phrases are also the titles of two successful books, written by Gillian McKeith and the psychiatrist Dr Richard Mackarness respectively, both of whom have been alternately hailed as cranks and pioneers. What is increasingly accepted by both medical and therapeutic communities is that there are connections between mental health and eating habits. We are not trying to say that if you eat in a healthy way you will never encounter stress, depression or other emotional difficulties. However, you can help yourself emotionally by thinking about what goes into your body.

We have divided this overview of healthy eating into two sections. The first reminds you of the *way* we should plan our eating, and the second looks at possible direct *connections* between certain nutrients, the foods they are found in and our mental well-being.

One of the main difficulties in implementing change is that when we feel low we haven't got the energy to change. Yet even small changes can help our mood. The main problems when we feel down in relation to our eating may be that:

- we overeat;
- we undereat;
- we eat 'badly' as we cannot be bothered to think about what we eat.

The way we eat

Much has been written about food and nutrition, but often we either let it go in one ear and out the other, or we pay attention for a while then drift back into old ways. Even if you already regularly pay attention to what you eat, there may still be some new ideas here.

Food intake affects our mood and behaviour. If you are hungry, you may be irritable and restless, even if you have trained your mind not to notice the hunger pangs. Often people are calmer and have a better sense of well-being after a meal – assuming they take time to eat, and don't simply eat a snack on the run!

Our brains need nutrients, and changes in levels of their intake can affect the neurotransmitters in our brains. These neurotransmitters can influence mood, sleep patterns and thinking. Deficiencies, or indeed excesses, of certain vitamins and minerals can damage nerves in the brain, and that may cause memory issues and affect problem-solving abilities.

Start the day well

You may not feel hungry or you may believe you haven't time to eat in the morning, but think about the word 'breakfast' – it is really two words, 'break' and 'fast'. That is just what we are doing, having fasted all night. It is hard to maintain stable blood sugar levels and effective functioning if we don't eat in the morning, so think how you can make this easy for yourself. Some ways might be:

- Prepare as much as you can the night before – maybe make a protein-filled sandwich with wholegrain bread and hard boiled egg.
- Drink a muesli smoothie.
- Eat a sugar-free nut and grain bar.
- If you really can only face a drink and not any food, make a milky drink (preferably with skimmed or semi-skimmed milk).

Continue to eat regularly during the day

The majority of people feel better if they eat at mealtimes and not in between. If you know you overeat when anxious, only cook the amount that you (and the family) will eat, otherwise you will be tempted to 'finish it up' and will put on weight over a period. Excess weight can make you lethargic and change your self-esteem. If someone else cooks your meals, talk to them about portion size. If you tend to undereat, then sometimes small things like making the food look attractive on the plate or going for your favourite (healthy!) foods can help you finish a meal.

Snacking or 'grazing' during the day is not usually a healthy way of eating, as often snacks are high in fat, sugar and salt. We also are less likely to eat well-balanced meals at mealtimes, as we are not hungry. There are some exceptions to this rule. If you are finding it difficult to eat enough to maintain a healthy weight at mealtimes and have tried different ways of doing this, or if you experience blood sugar lows, then snacking may be acceptable. However, if you do fall into this group, snack healthily and don't use it as an excuse to eat chocolate, crisps or buns all day! Go for protein-rich snacks, fruit or granola bars. Doing this can help you avoid dips in blood sugar level and resultant mood swings and fatigue.

The last thing to say is that it's not a good idea to eat late at night, close to going to bed. Your system hasn't had time to digest your meal, and you are likely to find sleep difficult or disturbed, which doesn't help your mental well-being. You could try a milky drink before bedtime.

What to drink?

The obvious thing to avoid is using alcohol to change mood. While initially alcohol can seem to lift our mood, it is in fact a depressant and makes our low moods even lower. It also adds unnecessary calories to our diet, so drink in moderation and avoid 'binge drinking'. Alcohol also can prevent the absorption of some nutrients into the body.

A good rule for many people is 'no caffeine after 4 p.m.' Caffeine stays active in our bodies for about six hours, so can interfere with our sleep. If you drink cola, go for light, caffeine-free varieties. Apart from affecting our sleep, caffeine also appears to sap water out of our systems, so is a bit like 'un-drinking'! Find no-added-sugar drinks that you like, or even plain water. Remember there is caffeine in tea and chocolate drinks as well as coffee, so see if you can at least replace these with caffeine-free brands.

Do drink plenty during the day, as this helps keep our systems healthy and that in itself can improve mood.

Nutrients and mental well-being

It is important to say that no nutrient is good or bad – it is the way we eat them that helps or hinders our well-being.

Carbohydrates

Carbohydrates are found in starchy foods like bread, rice, pasta, cereals, starchy vegetables and sugary foods such as cakes, puddings, biscuits, soft drinks and sweets. A meal high in carbohydrates will release insulin into the body, which enables us to use blood sugar from carbohydrates to release energy. Insulin also may indirectly affect serotonin levels in the brain. It is thought that this can enhance mood and also help reduce obsessive behaviours. However, a high sugar level may also cause hyperactivity, and as starches are often eaten with fat (chips, bread and butter, etc.), excessive intake is likely to cause weight problems.

Proteins

Proteins are found in meats, eggs and dairy products. They are also found in pulses (beans and peas), grains, nuts and seeds. Vegetarians must ensure that they blend these latter sources of protein in dishes to produce high-quality protein. Again, research suggests that amino acids that make up proteins may affect brain functioning and therefore mental well-being. It is therefore important that your meals contain a serving of protein alongside carbohydrates (meat and potatoes, bread and cheese, etc.). This is because if protein is eaten by itself, the body will use it to produce energy rather than using it for its primary function.

Fats

Fats are found in dairy foods and plant oils. There is a need to balance fat intake carefully. Too much leads to increased weight and potentially cholesterol increases in the body. On the other hand, there are studies that indicate that reducing the levels of fat intake too much could be connected with mood changes, anger and aggressive behaviour. Recently there has been much publicity about the benefits of omega-3, found in fish oils. It is suggested that omega-3 may be helpful with stress and bipolar affective disorder, though results are as yet inconclusive. Plant oils are generally considered to be healthier than animal fats.

Vitamins

Some vitamins are closely connected with mental well-being, in particular the vitamin B complex. For example,

- Lack of thiamine is linked with irritability, sleep disorders and fatigue (thiamine is obtained from pork, beans, peas, nuts, grains and the internal organs of animals).
- Lack of vitamin B12 is linked with nerve damage and brain atrophy (B12 is found only in foods of animal origin, so vegans may have to take a supplement).
- Lack of folic acid may be linked with depression (folic acid is found in liver, yeast, wheat and some nuts).
- Lack of niacin may cause loss of sleep, headaches and emotional instability (niacin is obtained from grains, meat, fish and peanuts).
- Lack of vitamin B6 is linked with depression and anxiety, but a deficiency is rare (B6 is found in many plant and animal foods).

Minerals

Minerals on the whole are not linked by strong research to mental well-being, other than the fact that a lack of iron, zinc and selenium in the diet may cause fatigue and irritability. A well-balanced healthy diet will avoid this occurring.

Allergies

While for most people the main considerations are around achieving a well-balanced diet so that deficiencies do not cause lows in our moods, for a few individuals allergies and reactions to specific foods could be linked to depression. There is some evidence that a wheat intolerance may occasionally cause this. Unfortunately, we are often intolerant to foods we enjoy. If you have any inkling that low mood or anxiety could be linked to what you are eating, it might be worth considering discussing this with your GP.

Conclusion

Your stress and worry levels, sleep habits, exercise and eating patterns all make major contributions to your mental health and well-being. Many of us find regulating them a significant challenge. Adopting a sensible, proactive approach, as suggested in this chapter, can bring many rewards in terms of good health.

Our hope is that having read through this book you are now feeling more confident, either in your own ability to cope by yourself with any emotional or psychological problem or distress you may have, or about making the decision to seek professional help. If you do decide to go ahead and arrange to see a therapist, you can do so now with more understanding and confidence about your own part in the process. If you prepare well, invest in and commit to therapy, you will be the richer for it.

Useful addresses

The following list of self-help material and links pertains to the promotion of mental health and well-being. It is a guide to encourage more self-reliance and resilience and can also serve as a useful aid in the course of your therapy.

Alcohol Concern
64 Leman Street
London E1 8EU
Tel.: 020 7264 0510; Drinkline: 0800 917 8282 (if you are concerned about your drinking or someone else's)
Website: www.alcoholconcern.co.uk

B-eat (Beating Eating Disorders)
103 Prince of Wales Road
Norwich NR1 1DW
Tel.: 0845 634 1414 (helpline)
Website: www.b-eat.co.uk

A specialist organization aimed at helping those with eating-related problems. They have an online contact service.

British Pain Society
The Secretariat
3rd Floor, Churchill House
35 Red Lion Square
London WC1R 4SG
Tel.: 020 7269 7840
Website: www.britishpainsociety.org

The largest multidisciplinary professional organization in the field of pain in the UK.

Cruse Bereavement Care
PO Box 800
Richmond
Surrey TW9 2RG
Tel.: 0844 477 9400 (helpline); 020 8939 9530 (admin)
Website: www.crusebereavementcare.org.uk

Provides telephone support and face-to-face counselling, often in a client's home; free leaflets on a range of information are also available.

DrugScope
Prince Consort House

Suite 204, 2nd Floor
109/111 Farringdon Road
London EC1R 3BW
Tel.: 020 7520 7550
Website: www.drugscope.org.uk

An independent centre for matters related to drugs, and the national
membership organization for all those involved in this field.

Mind (National Association for Mental Health)
15–19 Broadway
Stratford
London E15 4BQ
Tel.: 020 8519 2122
Mind*info*line: 0845 7660163 (9 a.m. to 5 p.m., Monday to Friday)
Website: www.mind.org.uk

There are local branches in England and Wales (the Welsh
headquarters is in Cardiff). Information and self-help on mental
health and related issues may be downloaded from the website (some
information is translated). There are interactive resources on the
website, as also for their section dedicated to young people, www.
youngminds.org.uk.

NHS Direct
Tel.: 0845 4647 (24hr, 365 days a year health enquiry line)
Website: www.nhsdirect.nhs.uk

General health website and encyclopaedia.

PACE
34 Hartham Road
London N7 9JL
Tel.: 020 7700 1323
Website: www.pacehealth.org.uk

Promotes the mental health and emotional well-being of the lesbian, gay,
bisexual and transgender community.

Parentline Plus
520 Highgate Studios
53–79 Highgate Road
Kentish Town
London NW5 1TL
Tel.: 020 7284 5500; helpline 0808 800 2222
Website: www.parentlineplus.org.uk

Provides a wide range of resources and help on all aspects of parenting
and childcare in general. The organization has eight local offices around

England as well as its London one, and the website includes a message board and discussion forum.

Phobic Action
Claybury Grounds
Manor Road
Woodford Green
Essex IG8 8PR
Tel.: 020 8506 0600

This national organization provides support and advice for those living with a variety of phobias. It has no website but may be contacted by letter or phone.

Relate
Premier House
Carolina Court
Lakeside
Doncaster DN4 5RA
Tel.: 0300 100 1234
Website: www.relate.org.uk

Relate started life in 1943 as the Marriage Guidance Council. It offers a well developed website with a range of information. Counselling can be face to face, online or by phone. Relate covers England and Wales; Scotland's website is www.relationships-scotland.org.uk

SAD (Seasonal Affective Disorder) Association
PO Box 989
Steyning
West Sussex BN44 3HG
Website: www.sada.org.uk

If writing, please enclose s.a.e.

Samaritans
PO Box 9090
Stirling
FK8 2SA
Tel.: 0845 90 90 90 (national helpline, 24 hrs a day every day)
Website: www.samaritans.org
Email: jo@samaritans.org

Samaritans help those who are coping with suicidal feelings or in distress or despair. As well as by phone and website, they can be approached by letter, and Samaritans also offers face-to-face counselling in their branches which are all over the UK and Ireland. For callers outside the UK, the website is www.befrienders.org

Professional organizations where you can find a therapist or counsellor

British Association for Behavioural and Cognitive Psychotherapies
Imperial House
Hornby Street
Bury
Lancashire BL9 5BN
Tel.: 0161 705 4304
Website: www.babcp.com

British Association for Counselling and Psychotherapy
BACP House
15 St John's Business Park
Lutterworth
Leicestershire LE17 4HB
Tel.: 01455 883300
Website: www.bacp.co.uk

British Psychological Society
St Andrew's House
48 Princess Road East
Leicester LE1 7DR
Tel.: 0116 254 9568
Website: www.bps.org.uk

United Kingdom Council for Psychotherapy
Second Floor, Edward House
2 Wakley Street
London EC1V 7LT
Tel.: 020 7014 9977
Website: www.psychotherapy.org.uk

See further under 'Interactive resources: Counselling'

Interactive resources (in addition to those mentioned above)

Addiction to alcohol/drugs
www.addictionnetwork.co.uk
www.addaction.org.uk
www.alcoholics-anonymous.org.uk
www.al-anonuk.org.uk (for families affected by)
www.12steptreatmentcentres.com

Addiction to gambling
www.gamaid.com
www.gamblersanonymous.org.uk

Gamcare: www.gamcare.org.uk
Offers support, information and advice to anyone suffering through a gambling problem, either online or via helpline 0845 6000 133 (8 a.m. to 2 a.m., every day.

Carers

www.carers.org

Counselling

Association for Counselling and Therapy Online: http://acto-uk.org
Contains a directory of counsellors plus more information for clients about counselling online.

Mindfulness-Based Cognitive Therapy: www.mbct.co.uk

Depression and mental health

Depression Alliance: www.depressionalliance.org

The National Autistic Society: www.autism.org.uk

SANE: www.sane.org.uk
A charity committed to helping people living with issues of mental health, and their families. SANEline (0845 767 8000) is open from 6 p.m. to 11 p.m., 365 days a year.

Eating disorders

National Centre for Eating Disorders: www.eating-disorders.org.uk
Provides a free newsletter and a range of information; clients are able to contact specialist counsellors who advertise on the site.

Men Get Eating Disorders Too: www.mengetedstoo.co.uk

Sexual abuse

The Survivors Trust: www.thesurvivorstrust.org
A national umbrella agency for over 100 specialist voluntary-sector agencies providing a wide range of support services for survivors of all forms of sexual abuse.

Young people

Beat Bullying: www.beatbullying.org
This organization works with children and young people across the UK to help those so deeply affected by bullying, both cyber- and real-world, that they can hardly face going to school; in addition, members aim to change the attitudes of those who do the bullying. This is done through a range of programmes involving peer mentoring and peer activism, mainly online and via mobile phone.

Child Bereavement Charity: www.childbereavement.org.uk
This serves both client and counsellor. A particular feature is the forum
where a child can register and talk about feelings to other bereaved
children. There is also a confidential support and information phone line.

ChildLine: www.childline.org.uk
In addition to using the helpline 0800 1111, a child can contact via email,
text and online chat.

Children of Addicted Parents and People: www.coap.co.uk
This website is run by volunteers for young people affected by someone
else's addiction to drugs, alcohol or some sort of behaviour such as
gambling.

Winston's Wish: www.winstonswish.org.uk
This childhood bereavement charity provides services to bereaved
children, young people and their families. There is also a national helpline
offering support and guidance to all those caring for children and young
people who have been bereaved: 08452 03 04 05.

Various

www.divorce-online.co.uk

www.redundancyhelp.co.uk

UK Self-Help Directory: www.ukselfhelp.info
A list of links for a huge variety of conditions, physical and mental. Some
links also lead to relevant book lists.

Ways Forward Counselling and Coaching: www.waysforward.com
A programme designed for adults (18-plus) who want to think through any
problem or concern in their personal, marital or professional lives.

Online self-help websites (in addition to those mentioned above)

The BBC provides information and interactive self-help programmes on
their following websites:
www.bbc.co.uk/health/emotional_health/mental_health/
www.bbc.co.uk/health/physical_health/family/

Channel Four: www.channel4.com/health also provides mental health
information, personal experiences and support on a wide variety of topics.

Living Life to the Full: www.livinglifetothefull.com
This site provides free access to an online mental-health life skills course
which has been developed by Chris Williams, a psychiatrist based in
Glasgow who has developed a CBT model known as the 'Five Areas
Approach'.

Mental Health Foundation: www.mentalhealth.org.uk
Information is provided on how to get help and general information on mental health: these include an A–Z of mental health; specific problems, issues and treatment; and news articles. There are also various interactive resources, including bulletin boards and forums for discussion on mental-health issues, and personal stories are published. The Foundation is also developing a campaign about the effectiveness of mindfulness meditation: see <www.bemindful.co.uk>.

Moodgym: www.moodgym.anu.edu.au
This site has been developed in Australia and is available free of charge. It uses CBT and Interpersonal Therapy approaches in the management of mental-health problems.

MultiKulti: www.multikulti.org.uk
Health information matters are translated into a range of languages.

Northumberland, Tyne and Wear: www.ntw.nhs.uk/pic/
This local authority's NHS Foundation Trust is one of the largest mental-health and disability trusts in England. The site offers a range of self-help booklets, and some information is translated.

Further reading

Aiken, Cara, *Surviving Post-natal Depression,* Jessica Kingsley, 2000.

Davies, William, *Overcoming Anger and Irritability,* Robinson, 2009.

Dryden, Dr Windy, *Overcoming Anxiety,* Sheldon Press, 2000.

Dryden, Dr Windy and Opie, Sarah, *Overcoming Depression,* Sheldon Press, 2003.

Faber, A. and Mazlish, E., *How To Talk so Kids Will Listen and Listen so Kids Will Talk,* Piccadilly Press, new edn, 2001.

Faber, A. and Mazlish, E., *How To Talk so Teens Will Listen and Listen so Teens Will Talk,* Piccadilly Press, 2006.

Gilbert, Paul, *Overcoming Depression,* Robinson, new revised edn, 2000.

Gournay, Professor Kevin, *Coping with Phobias and Panic,* Sheldon Press, 2010.

Greenberger, Dennis and Padesky, Christine A., *Mind Over Mood,* Guilford Press, 1995.

Hare, Jenny, *Free Your Life From Fear,* Sheldon Press, 2005.

Hawkins, Margaret, *Overcoming Panic and Related Anxiety Disorders,* Sheldon Press, 2009.

Isaac, M. and Marks, D. M., *Living with Fear,* McGraw-Hill, 2005.

Kennerley, Helen, *Overcoming Anxiety,* Robinson, 2009.

Quilliam, Susan, *Staying Together: From crisis to deeper commitment* (Relate Guide series), Vermilion, 2001.

Schmidt, Ulrike and Treasure, Janet, *Getting Better Bit(e) by Bit(e),* Psychology Press, 1993.

Silove, Derrick and Manicavasagar, Vijaya, *Overcoming Panic,* Robinson, 1997.

Treasure, Janet, *Anorexia Nervosa: A survival guide for families, friends and sufferers,* Psychology Press, 1997.

Trickett, Shirley, *Coping Successfully with Panic Attacks,* Sheldon Press, 2009.

Williams, Chris, *Overcoming Anxiety,* Hodder Arnold, 2003.

Williams, Chris, *Overcoming Depression,* Hodder Arnold, 2001.

Williams, Mark, Teasdale, John, Segal, Zindel and Kabat-Zinn, Jon, *The mindful way through Depression: Freeing yourself from chronic unhappiness,* The Guilford Press, 2007

Index